WORLD CUP
QUIZ BOOK!

Published in 2010 by BBC Books, an imprint of Ebury Publishing.
A Random House Group Company

Copyright © Match of the Day Magazine 2010

The Random House Group Limited Reg. No. 954009

Addresses for companies within the Random House Group can be found at
www.randomhouse.co.uk

A CIP catalogue record for this book is available from the British Library.

ISBN 978 1 84 607901 6

The Random House Group Limited supports the Forest Stewardship Council (FSC), the
leading international forest certification organisation. All our titles that are printed
on Greenpeace approved FSC certified paper carry the FSC logo. Our paper
procurement policy can be found at www.rbooks.co.uk/environment

Editor: Ian Foster
Content Editor: Richard Clare
Commissioning Editor: Albert DePetrillo
Project Editor: Caroline McArthur
Art Editor: Lee Gavigan
Designer: Mat Mannion
Production Editor: Neil Queen
Production: Phil Spencer
Sub-Editor: Dave Johnson
Junior Sub-Editor: Ravi Meah
Repro Technician: Robert James
Cover pictures: PA Photos

Printed and bound in the UK by Cox & Wyman

To buy books by your favourite authors and register for offers,
visit www.rbooks.co.uk

WELCOME!

Dear footy fan,

Congratulations on getting your hands on the best football quiz book around – it's bulging with questions on the world's hottest stars and the biggest tournament in world footy!

Challenge your mates and relatives to make the World Cup come alive!

Enjoy!

Match of the Day magazine team

MYSTERY MOBILE!

Which superstar owns this mobile phone? 50 points if you get it right!

DUDE! HOW'S EVERYTHING AT LIVERPOOL?

LET'S MEET! HAVEN'T SEEN YOU SINCE WE WERE AT POMPEY!

HI M8, CAN I BORROW UR LOTTO FOOTY BOOTS?

GUD LUCK WIV ENGLAND AT THE WORLD CUP BUD!

YOU LEFT YOUR NO.2 SHIRT AT MY PAD, YOU DOUGHNUT!

WHO IS IT?

....

MY SCORE...
OUT OF 50

MY MATE'S...

MY DAD'S...

TEAM SHEET!

Fill in the gaps and get ten points for each one!

2010 WORLD CUP GROUP C
ENGLAND V USA
SATURDAY 12 JUNE

ENGLAND

Robert	GK	West Ham
Glen JOHNSON	DF	....
Ashley COLE	DF	Chelsea
... FERDINAND (C)	DF	Man. United
John TERRY	DF	Chelsea
Gareth	MF	Man. City
..... LENNON	MF	Tottenham
Frank LAMPARD	MF	Chelsea
Steven GERRARD	MF	Liverpool
Jermain DEFOE	..	Tottenham
Wayne ROONEY	ST	Man. United

USA

Tim HOWARD	GK	....
Carlos BOCANEGRA (C)	DF	Rennes
Oguchi ONYEWU	DF	AC Milan
Steve CHERUNDOLO	DF	Hannover
Jonathan BORNSTEIN	DF	Chivas USA
Maurice EDU	MF	Rangers
Michael BRADLEY	MF	B. M'gladbach
Stuart HOLDEN	MF	Bolton
..... DEMPSEY	MF	Fulham
Landon DONOVAN	ST	LA Galaxy
Jozy ALTIDORE	ST	Hull

SUBSTITUTES

Peter CROUCH, Wes BROWN,
..... MILNER, David BECKHAM,
David JAMES

SUBSTITUTES

Brad GUZAN, Jonathan SPECTOR,
Robbie ROGERS, Jose Francisco
TORRES, Kenny COOPER

MANAGER Fabio ....

MANAGER Bob BRADLEY

MY SCORE... OUT OF 100

MY MATE'S... MY DAD'S.

7

LIONEL MESSI!

Ten points for each right answer on the superstar!

1 What shirt number does Messi wear for Argentina?

A 9
B 10 ⃝
C 23

2 Which boots does Messi wear?

A Adidas
B Nike ⃝
C Umbro

3 Which Barca boss gave Messi his senior debut?

A Terry Venables
B Frank Rijkaard ⃝
C Sir Bobby Robson

4 He scored in last year's Champions League final – but against which side?

A Real Madrid
B Man. United ⃝
C Chelsea

5 When did he make his debut for Barcelona?

A 1999 ⃝
B 2004
C 2010

6 How many games has Messi played for Barcelona?

A 0-50
B 51-100
C 101-150

7 In which year was Messi named World Player of the Year?

A 2007 B 2008 **C 2009** ⃝

8 True or false – Messi went to the 2006 World Cup in Germany!

A True B False

9 When did he win an Olympic gold medal with Argentina?

A 2004
B 2008
C 2000

10 Leo's birthday is on 24 June – how old will he be this year?

A 19 **B 23** ⃝ C 27

MY SCORE... **OUT OF 100**

MY MATE'S...

MY DAD'S...

8

ANSWERS ON PAGE 201 (DON'T CHEAT!)

SIL-WHO-ETTE!

Can you identify these MOTD experts?
It's 25 points for each right answer!

WHO IS IT?

1. Gray Linker

WHO IS IT?

2. ....

MY SCORE... OUT OF 50

MY MATE'S... MY DAD'S...

MEGA WORDSEARCH!

Can you find the 20 top players that are hiding below? It's five points for each name you can find!

Benzema

Drogba

Dzeko

Eto'o

Fabiano

Forlan

Frei

Gomes

Henry

Huntelaar

Klose

Martins

Rooney

Santa Cruz

Tevez

Toni

Torres

Van Persie

Vela

Villa

R	N	T	O	P	O	F	U	O	E	I	A	F	E	A
D	Z	E	K	O	D	N	P	S	E	M	O	G	L	A
E	I	S	R	E	P	N	A	V	E	R	E	L	R	M
D	R	O	G	B	A	E	F	I	L	I	I	S	N	E
A	L	E	V	N	A	R	U	A	B	V	E	I	I	Z
Y	R	N	E	H	E	S	N	O	Y	A	E	E	R	N
S	T	O	C	I	A	R	S	T	O	E	F	Y	R	E
E	S	O	L	K	Z	U	R	C	A	T	N	A	S	B
R	G	P	E	C	I	T	S	E	G	M	E	O	T	S
R	A	A	L	E	T	N	U	H	N	O	O	O	O	H
O	T	U	O	S	I	T	E	V	E	Z	P	N	N	R
T	D	W	O	T	G	R	E	A	M	R	E	K	I	T
C	A	D	R	O	R	P	A	N	T	F	R	C	T	R
S	A	A	A	Y	F	X	R	D	Y	R	H	O	R	H
G	M	I	L	R	O	T	I	E	M	L	D	T	L	A

MY SCORE... OUT OF 100

MY MATE'S...

MY DAD'S...

TRANSFER CONNECT!

Match these World Cup stars with the transfer fees they were bought for – it's 25 points for each one you get right!

1 RONALDO
Portugal winger
Man. United to Real Madrid
£ _80 million_

2 GIANLUIGI BUFFON
Italy keeper
Parma to Juventus
£ __25 milli__

3 GLEN JOHNSON
England defender
Portsmouth to Liverpool
£ __18 million__

4 CARLOS TEVEZ
Argentina forward
Man. United to Man. City
£ __32 million__

A £18M   B £25M   C £80M   D £32M

MY SCORE... **OUT OF 100**
MY MATE'S...   MY DAD'S...

PREM LINK!

Match these wicked World Cup stars with their Prem clubs! Ten points for each correct answer!

1 WILLIAM GALLAS
Country: FRANCE
Club: Tottenham
....

2 MARK SCHWARZER
Country: AUSTRALIA
Club: Fulam
....

3 KOLO TOURE
Country: IVORY COAST
Club: Man.C
....

4 JOSEPH YOBO
Country: NIGERIA
Club: Everton
....

5 PEPE REINA
Country: SPAIN
Club: Leverpool
....

6 NADIR BELHADJ
Country: ALGERIA
Club: Portsmou
....

7 JERMAIN DEFOE
Country: ENGLAND
Club: Tottenham
....

8 JOHN OBI MIKEL
Country: NIGERIA
Club: chelsea
....

9 PARK JI-SUNG
Country: SOUTH KOREA
Club: Man.U
....

10 JOZY ALTIDORE
Country: USA
Club: Hull
....

TOTTENHAM
MAN. UNITED
ARSENAL
LIVERPOOL
CHELSEA
HULL
FULHAM
MAN. CITY
EVERTON
PORTSMOUTH

☐ MY SCORE... **OUT OF 100**
☐ MY MATE'S... ☐ MY DAD'S...

WAYNE ROONEY!

1 Where did Rooney join Man. United from?

A Man. City
B Everton ✓
C Liverpool

2 Wayne won the 2008 Champions League – who did United beat in the final?

A Barcelona
B Chelsea ✓
C Arsenal

3 True or false – Rooney was sent off at the last World Cup!

A True ✓ B False

4 What number does he wear for England?

A 8 B 9 C 10 ✓

5 What is Wayne's wife called?

A Coleen
B Abbey
C Cheryl

MY SCORE...

JUMBLED UP!

1 ROPTAGUL
Portugal

2 ECHIL
Chile ✓

3 REECEG
Greece

4 LANDGEN
England

5 NARFCE
France

6 NAPJA
Japan

It's ten points each for each right answer on the England star!

6 Which footy boots does Wazza wear?

A Nike ✓
B Umbro
C Puma

7 Cristiano Ronaldo wants Wayne to join him at which club?

A Real Valladolid
B Real Madrid
C Atletico Madrid

8 Against which club did Rooney score a hat-trick on his United debut?

A Fenerbahce
B Torquay ✓
C Getafe

9 What name did he give to his son, who was born last year?

A Pie ✓ B Sky C Kai

10 Rooney made his Man. United debut under which manager?

A Steve Bruce
B Harry Redknapp
C Sir Alex Ferguson

OUT OF 100 [ ] **MY MATE'S...** [ ] **MY DAD'S...**

Can you work out who these World Cup countries are? It's ten points for each one!

7 CEXIMO

mexico

8 GAYRUUU

9 SAU
USA

10 RONTH ROKEA
North Korea

MY SCORE... **OUT OF 100**
MY MATE'S... [ ] **MY DAD'S...**

15

10 QUESTIONS ON ENGLAND

Ten points for each correct answer!

1 With 125 appearances, who is England's most capped keeper ever?
- **A** David James
- **B** David Seaman ✓
- **C** Peter Shilton

2 Who is the vice-captain of the England team?
- **A** Rio Ferdinand
- **B** Frank Lampard
- **C** Steven Gerrard ✓

3 Which nationality is England coach Fabio Capello?
- **A** Italian ✓
- **B** French
- **C** Spanish

4 Where did Liverpool defender Glen Johnson start his footy career?
- **A** Portsmouth
- **B** West Ham
- **C** Chelsea ✓

5 Which of these England strikers has celebrated his goals with the robot dance?
- **A** Emile Heskey
- **B** Peter Crouch ✓
- **C** Jermain Defoe

6 In which position did MOTD presenter Gary Lineker play for England?
- **A** Defender
- **B** Midfielder
- **C** Striker ✓

7 In which year did Ashley Cole make his England debut?
- **A** 1991 **B** 1997 **C** 2001

8 How many World Cups has Wayne Rooney played in?
- **A** 1 **B** 0 **C** 2 ✓

9 Who will England play in their first World Cup game?
- **A** USA ✓
- **B** Slovenia
- **C** Algeria

10 How many goals did Theo Walcott score against Croatia in the qualifiers?
- **A** 1 **B** 2 ✓ **C** 3

MY SCORE... OUT OF 100

MY MATE'S...

MY DAD'S...

16

CROSSWORD FUN!

Ten points for each right answer!

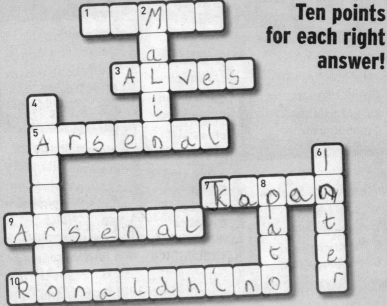

Across answers shown in grid:
- 1 (with 2 down) M
- 3 ALves
- 5 Arsenal
- 7 Kapan
- 9 Arsenal
- 10 Ronaldhino
- Down: Mail, Fabat, later (as handwritten)

ACROSS

1 Brazil's team nickname, The _____ Kings (5)
3 Flying Barcelona right-back, Dani _____ (5)
5 Gilberto Silva used to play for this Prem club (7)
7 Brazil won the 2002 World Cup in this country (5)
9 Robinho's Premier League club (3, 4)
10 Milan trickster who used to star for Barcelona (10)

DOWN

2 Italian club that sold Kaka to Real Madrid, AC _____ (5)
4 Sevilla goal-machine, Luis _____ (7)
6 Club that defender Maicon plays for, _____ Milan (5)
8 Brilliant young Milan striker, Alexandre _____ (4)

MY SCORE... **OUT OF 100**

MY MATE'S...

MY DAD'S...

17

10 QUESTIONS ON

Ten points for each correct answer!

1 Who is Spain's first-choice keeper?

A Rafael Nadal
B Iker Casillas ✓
C Gianluigi Buffon

2 At which Spanish club did Fernando Torres start his career?

A Real Madrid
B Real Zaragoza
C Atletico Madrid ✓

3 How old is Spain's long-haired scruffy centre-back Carles Puyol?

A 24 B 32 C 37

4 What is the nickname of Spain's national team?

A The Red Fury
B The Angry Reds
C The Moody Reds

5 How many goals did David Villa score in seven World Cup qualifying games?

A 1 B 4 C 7

MY SCORE...

COUNTRY CONNECT!

Match the countries

1 MICHAEL BALLACK — F

2 BACARY SAGNA — I

3 CARLOS TEVEZ — J

4 NEMANJA VIDIC — E

5 WILSON PALACIOS — H

6 JAMES MILNER — B

7 STEVEN PIENAAR — C

8 ALBERTO AQUILANI — A

9 MICHAEL ESSIEN — G

10 TIM CAHILL — D

SPAIN!

6 What is the name of Spain's well podgy team manager?
- **A** Vincent Vega
- **B** Vicente del Bosque ✓
- **C** Leonardo da Vinci

7 Which Spanish player did Wayne Rooney describe as the best in the world?
- **A** Andres Iniesta
- **B** Xavi
- **C** Sergio Ramos ✓

8 Who did Spain beat in the final of Euro 2008, with a goal from Fernando Torres?
- **A** France
- **B** Italy
- **C** Germany ✓

9 How many times have Spain won the World Cup?
- **A** 0 ✓ **B** 2 **C** 3

10 Which shirt number does the Spain midfielder Cesc Fabregas wear for Arsenal?
- **A** 4 ✓ **B** 10 **C** 14

OUT OF 100 [ ] **MY MATE'S...** [ ] **MY DAD'S...**

World Cup stars with their World Cup – it's ten points for each correct answer!

- **A** ITALY
- **B** ENGLAND
- **C** S. AFRICA
- **D** AUSTRALIA
- **E** SERBIA
- **F** GERMANY
- **G** GHANA
- **H** HONDURAS
- **I** FRANCE
- **J** ARGENTINA

[ ] **MY SCORE...** **OUT OF 100**

[ ] **MY MATE'S...** [ ] **MY DAD'S...**

19

TEAM BUS CHALLENGE!

Four top World Cup stars are late for a game, but which route will lead them to the correct team bus? It's 25 points for each one you get right!

1 Lionel Messi 2 Wayne Rooney 3 Kaka 4 Cesc Fabregas

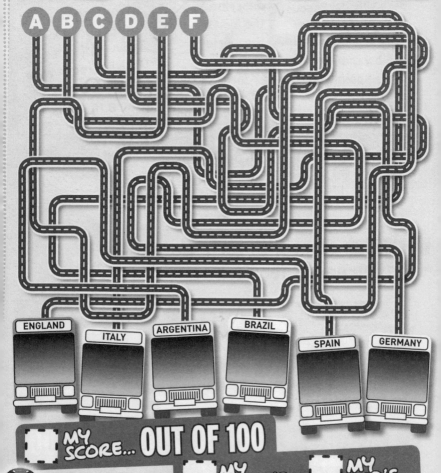

MY SCORE... **OUT OF 100**

MY MATE'S... MY DAD'S...

20

NICKNAME CONNECT!

Can you match up these World Cup stars with their nicknames? Take 20 points for each correct answer!

1 Fernando Torres D

A "TITI"

2 Thierry Henry A

B "THE BISON"

3 Michael Essien B

C "WAZZA"

4 Gianluigi Buffon E

D "EL NINO"

5 Wayne Rooney C

E "GIGI"

MY SCORE... **OUT OF 100**

MY MATE'S...   MY DAD'S...

21

CRISTIANO RONALDO!

Ten points for each right answer on the superstar!

1 At which club did Ron start his career?

A Benfica
B Sporting Lisbon ✓
C Arsenal

2 True or false – Ronaldo is the Portugal captain!

A True
B False ✓

3 Which boots does Ronaldo wear?

A Adidas ✓
B Puma
C Nike

4 Real Madrid broke the world transfer record to buy him – but how much did they pay?

A £60 million
B £80 million ✓
C £100 million

5 How many goals did he bag to win the Prem Golden Boot in 2008?

A 21 B 26 ✓ C 31

6 How many World Cups has he played in for Portugal?

A 0 B 1 C 2 ✓

7 In which year was he named World Player of the Year?

A 2007 B 2008 ✓ C 2009

8 How many Prem games did he play for United between 2003 and 2009?

A 196
B 133 ✓
C 79

9 Ron has followed David Beckham by modelling for which fashion brand?

A Armani
B Donnay
C Lonsdale

10 What shirt number does Ronaldo wear at Real Madrid?

A 7 B 10 C 9 ✓

MY SCORE...

OUT OF 100

MY MATE'S... MY DAD'S...

WHO AM I?

Can you work out this top star from their clues? 50 points if you're right!

I play for a London club!

I wear the shirt number 52 for my club!

I'll be playing up front for my country in the World Cup!

I once played for Birmingham on loan!

I had a bad hamstring injury earlier this season!

I've worn pink footy boots in the past!

I'm only 22 years old!

Mates call me Nikki B!

WHO IS IT?

.... Nicholas Bendtner

MY SCORE... OUT OF 50

MY MATE'S... MY DAD'S...

23

TEAM SHEET!

Fill in the gaps and get ten points for each one!

2010 WORLD CUP GROUP G
BRAZIL v IVORY COAST
SUNDAY 20 JUNE

BRAZIL

Julio CESAR	GK	*Inter* Milan
Dani	DF	Barcelona
MAICON	DF	Inter Milan
LUCIO (C)	DF	Inter Milan
LUISAO	DF	Benfica
Felipe MELO	MF	Juventus
GILBERTO	MF	Panathinaikos
KAKA	MF	*Real Madrid*
ELANO	MF	Galatasaray
ROBINHO	*M.F*	Man. City
Luis FABIANO	ST	Sevilla

SUBSTITUTES

VICTOR, Thiago SILVA, LUCAS, HULK, Alexandre PATO

MANAGER

DUNGA

IVORY COAST

Boubacar BARRY	GK	Lokeren
Siaka TIENE	DF	Valenciennes
Kolo TOURE	DF	*Manchester*
.... EBOUE	DF	Arsenal
Sol BAMBA	DF	Hibernian
Didier ZOKORA	MF	Sevilla
.... TOURE	MF	Barcelona
Cheik TIOTE	MF	Twente
Salomon KALOU	ST	*Chelsea*
Abdel Kader KEITA	*MF*	Galatasaray
Didier ...... (C)	ST	Chelsea

SUBSTITUTES

Vincent ANGBAN, Abdoulaye MEITE, Emerse FAE, Aruna DINDANE, GERVINHO

MANAGER

Sven GORAN ERIKSSON

MY MATE'S... MY DAD'S...

MY SCORE...OUT OF 100

CROSSWORD FUN!

Ten points for each right answer!

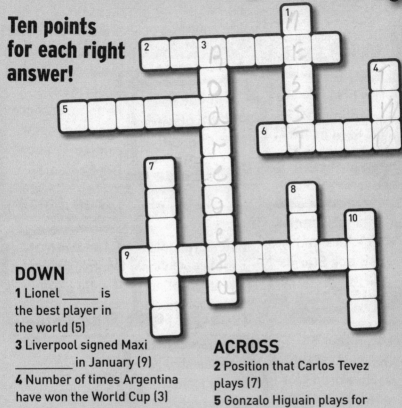

DOWN

1 Lionel _____ is the best player in the world (5)

3 Liverpool signed Maxi _____ in January (9)

4 Number of times Argentina have won the World Cup (3)

7 In which league does Sergio Aguero play in? (2, 4)

8 Number of times Argentina have won gold at the Olympic footy tournament (3)

10 Argentina's home shirt is white and light _____ (4)

ACROSS

2 Position that Carlos Tevez plays (7)

5 Gonzalo Higuain plays for Real _____ (6)

6 Argentina's mad gaffer _____ Maradona (5)

9 Javier Mascherano plays for this Prem club (9)

MY SCORE... **OUT OF 100**

MY MATE'S...

MY DAD'S...

25

TRUE OR FALSE?

Which facts are true and which are false? Circle the right answers – it's ten points for each one!

1 The first ever World Cup finals were held in 1810!

True **False**

2 Uruguay have no Prem players in their squad!

True **False**

3 Germany's national anthem uses the theme tune to TV show Big Brother!

True False

4 Ghana's team are nicknamed The Black Stars!

True False

5 Michael Carrick started his footy career at West Ham!

True **False**

6 The World Cup trophy is made of solid gold!

True False

7 This year's finals will see North Korea play in the World Cup for the first time!

True False

8 France striker Thierry Henry was named after a vacuum cleaner!

True False

9 This year is the first time an African country has hosted the World Cup!

True False

10 Arsenal striker Carlos Vela plays for Mexico!

True False

MY SCORE... **OUT OF 100**

MY MATE'S...

MY DAD'S...

QUALIFIED?

Put a tick next to the country that made it to South Africa or a cross if they didn't – ten points for each!

1 REP. OF IRELAND
Did they qualify?

2 GREECE
Did they qualify? ✓

3 CHILE
Did they qualify? ✓

4 RUSSIA
Did they qualify?

5 WALES
Did they qualify?

6 NIGERIA
Did they qualify? ✓

7 TOGO
Did they qualify?

8 COSTA RICA
Did they qualify?

9 PORTUGAL
Did they qualify? ✓

10 JAMAICA
Did they qualify?

MY SCORE... **OUT OF 100**

MY MATE'S...   MY DAD'S...

DADS V LADS

Get your dad to answer the questions on the left while you do the right – ten points for each correct answer!

1990

1 Which city hosted the 1990 World Cup final?

2 Who was England's captain for the semi-final against West Germany?

3 Name two of the three countries that were in England's group!

4 Who won the World Cup that year?

5 Who was England's first-choice keeper in 1990?

NOW

1 Which country will host this year's World Cup?

2 Who's the captain of the England team?

3 Name two of the three countries that are in England's group!

4 Who won the last World Cup in 2006?

5 Which English keeper will be 39 years old when the World Cup takes place?

MY DAD'S... OUT OF 50 MY SCORE...

NAME GAME!

Know who these players are? Fill in the missing letters on their shirts – 20 points for each kit!

R_ _NE_

10 ①

ENGLAND

_ABIA_O

② **9**

BRAZIL

CA_VA_ _O

③ **6**

PORTUGAL

ANNAVA _

④ **5**

ITALY

_AVI

8 ⑤

SPAIN

MY SCORE... **OUT OF 100**

MY MATE'S...   MY DAD'S...

29

DIDIER DROGBA!

Ten points for each right answer on the superstar!

1 Drogba joined Chelsea in 2004 from which club?

A Marseille ✓
B Auxerre
C Monaco

2 Which Blues manager signed him for Chelsea?

A Guus Hiddink
B Avram Grant
C Jose Mourinho ✓

3 Where did the Drog begin his pro footy career?

A Le Boys
B Le Mans ✓
C Le Womans

4 True or false – he's the captain of Ivory Coast!

A True ✓
B False

5 Which footy boots does Didier wear?

A Nike ✓
B Adidas
C Umbro

6 How many games has he played for Ivory Coast?

A 0-10
B 60-70
C 30-40 ✓

7 What shirt number does the Drog wear for Chelsea?

A 9 B 10 C 11 ✓

8 In which year did he win the Prem Golden Boot?

A 2007
B 2008
C 2009 ✓

9 How old is the superstar striker?

A 26 ✓
B 29
C 32

10 How many World Cup finals has Drogba played in before 2010?

A 0 ✓ B 1 C 2

 MY SCORE... **OUT OF 100**

MY MATE'S...   MY DAD'S...

 30

MYSTERY MOBILE!

Which superstar owns this mobile phone? 50 points if you get it right!

UR LATEST #5 MAGAZINE LOOKS AWESOME, DUDE!

HOW'S YOUR BROTHER ANTON DOING THESE DAYS?

AFTER UR PER4MANCE 2DAY I CAN C Y UNITED PAID £30M FOR U!

MATE! HOW'S UR BAD BACK NOW?

THE DEFENCE AIN'T THE SAME WITHOUT YOU OR TERRY AT THE BACK!

WHO IS IT?

....

MY SCORE...

OUT OF 50

MY MATE'S...

MY DAD'S...

31

MEGA WORDSEARCH!

Can you find the 20 England stars that are hiding below? It's five points for each name you find!

Barry

Bent

Brown

Carrick

Cole

Crouch

Defoe

Ferdinand

Gerrard

Green

Hart

Heskey

James

Johnson

Lampard

Lennon

Rooney

Terry

Upson

Walcott

```
F F R N Y O L M B S E H N N E
O E N R R T I F L N R E O L L
E N R E M T U H F N E N O A E
C E L D T N A T S R N C M S E
T A W T I E E N G E S P I E N
O T R A T N C E L H A T S M T
L T R R L M A B E R C N D A O
T T S E I C E N D T T U U J E
Y R R A B C O A D G T P O E T
R O O N E Y K T E N S H A R T
N O S N H O J R T O A B I T C
N D R V R T R W N O E R M E I
D A A E T A Y A O D O O U A R
F O O A R H E S K E Y W L I O
C E A D E O F E D U C N Y A T
```

MY SCORE... **OUT OF 100**

MY MATE'S... MY DAD'S...

Circle the odd one out in each of the boxes below – pick up 20 points for each right answer!

1
DAVID JAMES   IKER CASILLAS
BRAD FRIEDEL   GARETH BARRY

2
AARON LENNON   ALBERT RIERA
CRISTIANO RONALDO   FABIO CAPELLO

3
4-4-2   4-5-1
4-3-3   1-2-7

4
CESC FABREGAS   FERNANDO TORRES
XABI ALONSO   MICHAEL BALLACK

5
JERMAIN DEFOE   WAYNE ROONEY
EMILE HESKEY   RIO FERDINAND

MY SCORE... **OUT OF 100**
MY MATE'S...   MY DAD'S...

33

SIL-WHO-ETTE!

Can you identify MOTD experts are these?
It's 25 points for each right answer!

> Och, aye! The defending there was shocking!

> I'm alongside Jonathan Pearce in the commentary box here!

> HE PLAYED IN 621 GAMES FOR LIVERPOOL – WINNING EIGHT LEAGUE TITLES WITH THE REDS!

> HE HELPED CRYSTAL PALACE REACH THE 1990 FA CUP FINAL, AND PLAYED 135 GAMES FOR SHEFF. WED.!

WHO IS IT?

1...................

WHO IS IT?

2...................

MY SCORE... OUT OF 50

MY MATE'S...

MY DAD'S...

34

SOUTH AFRICA GUIDE

Ten points for each question answered correctly on the World Cup hosts!

1 In which city will the World Cup final be played?

A Iceberg
B Johannesburg ✓
C Hamburg

2 We use the pound, but which currency is used in South Africa?

A Bogey
B Rand
C Sand

SOUTH AFRICA HAS THREE OFFICIAL CAPITAL CITIES!

5 Which of these dudes is a famous South African?

A Sherlock Holmes
B The Stig
C Nelson Mandela ✓

3 Which of these places is a massive South African City?

A Cape Town ✓
B Pants Town
C Wellies Town

4 Which continent is South Africa in?

A America
B Asia
C Africa ✓

SOUTH AFRICA ARE THE CURRENT RUGBY WORLD CUP CHAMPIONS!

MY SCORE... **OUT OF 50**

MY MATE'S...

MY DAD'S...

35

FERNANDO TORRES!

Ten points for each right answer on the superstar!

1 In which of these finals did Torres score the winning goal?

A Euro 2004
B 2006 World Cup
C Euro 2008 ✓

2 How much did Liverpool buy him for in 2007?

A £10m+
B £20m+ ✓
C £30m+

3 How old is the Spanish striker?

A 20 B 26 ✓ C 32

6 How many matches has Torres played for Spain?

A 0-20
B 40-60
C 70-90

4 Torres started his career at which club?

A Real Madrid
B Atletico Madrid ✓
C Valencia

5 How many World Cups has Torres played in?

A 0 B 1 C 2 ✓

9 Which Liverpool gaffer brought him to Anfield?

A Roy Evans
B Gerard Houllier
C Rafa Benitez ✓

7 Which boots does he wear?

A Nike
B Adidas ✓
C Puma

8 What's tattooed on his right wrist?

A The number nine
B His face
C The Liverpool badge

10 His nickname is El Nino – but what does it mean?

A The Kid ✓
B The Meerkat
C Smiling Assassin

MY SCORE... **OUT OF 100**

MY MATE'S... MY DAD'S...

RAPPING ROWS!

Write the answers to the clues in the spaces below – they all rhyme. Grab 25 points for each group!

1 West Ham and England keeper Rob _bert green_
2 England's national anthem is God Save the _Queen_
3 Theo Walcott's shirt number at Arsenal _14_

4 Man. City and England midfielder Gareth _barry_
5 Match of the Day presenter _Grrey_ Lineker
6 Defoe has been managed at three different clubs by _harry_ Redknapp

7 France and Bayern Munich winger Franck _Ribery_
8 Surname of the current World Player of the Year _Kaka_
9 France and Barcelona striker Thierry _henry_

10 England's Italian gaffer Fabio _capells_
11 Portugal megastar Cristiano _Roinaldo_
12 Colour of South Africa's home shirt _yellow_

1	→2	→3
4	→5	→6
7	→8	→9
10	→11	→12

MY SCORE... **OUT OF 100**

MY MATE'S...   MY DAD'S...

PREM LINK!

Can you match these World Cup stars with their Prem clubs? Ten points for each correct answer!

1 PATRICE EVRA
Country: FRANCE
Club: Man U
....

2 SALOMON KALOU
Country: IVORY COAST
Club: Chelsea
....

3 KAMEL GHILAS
Country: ALGERIA
Club:
....

4 EMMANUEL EBOUE
Country: IVORY COAST
Club: Arsenal
....

5 NIGEL DE JONG
Country: HOLLAND
Club: Man C
....

6 PETER CROUCH
Country: ENGLAND
Club: Tottenham
....

7 AARON MOKOENA
Country: SOUTH AFRICA
Club:
....

8 LUCAS
Country: BRAZIL
Club:
....

9 JOHN PAINTSIL
Country: GHANA
Club:
....

10 ROBERT HUTH
Country: GERMANY
Club: Stoke
....

MAN. CITY
LIVERPOOL
MAN. UNITED
CHELSEA
HULL
STOKE
ARSENAL
FULHAM
TOTTENHAM
PORTSMOUTH

MY SCORE... **OUT OF 100**

MY MATE'S...   MY DAD'S...

TRUE OR FALSE?

Which facts are true and which are false? Circle the right answers – ten points per correct one!

1 Australia's nickname is the Socceroos!

True ~~False~~

2 Steve Bruce is the manager of Denmark!

True ~~False~~

3 This year's World Cup will be the 19th one!

True False

4 Blackburn defender Ryan Nelsen is the New Zealand captain!

True ~~False~~

5 Before this year, David Beckham had played in three World Cups!

~~True~~ **False**

6 Arsenal's Bacary Sagna plays for Italy!

True ~~False~~

7 Brazil's home shirt is white!

True ~~False~~

8 England haven't gone further than the quarter-finals since 1990!

~~True~~ **False**

9 This is the first year that the Republic of Ireland hasn't qualified!

~~True~~ **False**

10 Fernando Torres has played over 50 games for Portugal!

True ~~False~~

MY SCORE... **OUT OF 100**

MY MATE'S...

MY DAD'S...

39

10 QUESTIONS ON
Ten points for each correct answer!

1 Who is the Brazil captain?
- **A** Lucio ✓
- **B** Toileto
- **C** Bogo

2 Which Brazil star has celebrated scoring goals by sucking his thumb?
- **A** Julio Baptista
- **B** Robinho ✓
- **C** Hulk

3 Young striker Alexandre Pato plays for which club?
- **A** AC Milan ✓
- **B** Roma
- **C** Grimsby

4 How many times have Brazil won the World Cup?
- **A** 1
- **B** 3
- **C** 5 ✓

5 Who's the Brazilian gaffer?
- **A** Dunga ✓
- **B** Raymond Domenech
- **C** Fabio Capello

MY SCORE...

COUNTRY CONNECT!

Match the countries

1 FRANK LAMPARD
2 THIERRY HENRY — C
3 XABI ALONSO — A
4 BASTIAN SCHWEINSTEIGER — F
5 GONZALO HIGUAIN — B
6 GIANLUIGI BUFFON — C
7 SOTIRIOS KYRGIAKOS
8 NUNO GOMES
9 MARCUS HAHNEMANN
10 SAMUEL ETO'O — E

BRAZIL!

6 Who is Brazil's all-time top scorer?
A George Best
B Bobby Charlton
C Pele ✓

7 Which of these Prem keepers is Brazilian?
A Jussi Jaaskelainen
B Chris Kirkland
C Heurelho Gomes ✓

8 Awesome right-back Dani Alves plays for which club?
A Barcelona ✓
B Man. United
C Inter Milan

9 Which of these Samba stars plays for Real Madrid?
A Lucas
B Kaka ✓
C Luis Fabiano

10 Brazil's first ever match in 1914 was against which English team?
A Brentford
B Exeter
C Stockport

OUT OF 100 ☐ MY MATE'S... ☐ MY DAD'S...

orld Cup super stars with their World Cup
's ten points for each correct answer!

A SPAIN   **F** GERMANY   **H** USA

B ARGENTINA   **I** PORTUGAL

C ITALY   **G** FRANCE   **J** ENGLAND

D GREECE   ☐ MY SCORE... OUT OF 100

E CAMEROON   ☐ MY MATE'S...   ☐ MY DAD'S...

41

WHOSE INBOX?

Guess which star is receiving these emails – 50 points if you get it right!

1

Subject: Hola!
From: Nicklas
Sent: April 2010

Can I borrow your Nike footy boots this weekend? I've got a game and I've lost mine!

Thanks,
Tricky Nicky

P.S. You gotta teach me how to create goals like you some day!

2

Subject: <no subject>
From: Sol
Sent: April 2010

Hola Senor No.4!

You left your club captain's armband at my house, you muppet!

Catch you soon,
Sol

3

Subject: Good luck with Spain!
From: Carles
Sent: April 2010

Hey man,

Good luck breaking into the Spanish midfield this summer – Iniesta and Xavi are difficult to shift!

Have a good one,
C

4

Subject: Happy Birthday!
From: Theo
Sent: 4 May 2010

Happy 23rd birthday, wee man!

Good luck this summer – unless you come up against England ;-)

Theo

WHO IS IT?

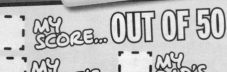

MY SCORE... OUT OF 50

MY MATE'S...   MY DAD'S...

42

SHOOTING PRACTICE!

Write your answers in the target to reveal a country around the outer letters – get 50 points if you find it!

TIP! Answers start from the outer edge and go towards the centre so that each one ends with the letter Y!

1. Roque Santa Cruz plays for this country (8)

2. Funny nickname of Juventus. It's also what your gran is! (3,4)

3. France and Bayern Munich winger Franck _____ (6)

4. England and Chelsea ace John _____ (5)

5. Country of Atletico Madrid striker Diego Forlan (7)

6. Michael Ballack captains this country (7)

7. England left-back _____ Cole (6)

8. _____ King – Spurs captain with 19 England caps (6)

Target letters shown: LEDLE, ASHLEY, Y, REBIR, GERMANA, ARRET, G, UGORU, T

COUNTRY NAME:

....

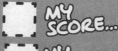

MY SCORE... **OUT OF 50**

MY MATE'S... MY DAD'S...

43

CROSSWORD FUN!

Get ten points for each right answer!

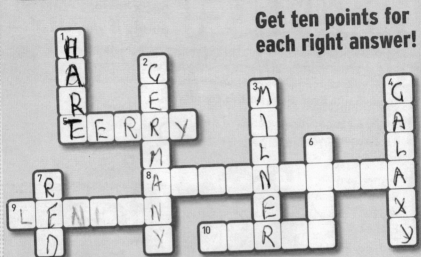

DOWN

1 Joe _____, who spent the season on loan at Birmingham (4)

2 England beat West _____ in the 1966 World Cup final (7)

3 Aston Villa midfielder James _____ (6)

4 David Beckham's US team is LA _____ (6)

6 Number of goals England scored against Croatia at home in qualifying (4)

7 Colour of England's new away shirt (3)

ACROSS

5 Surname of England and Chelsea star John _____ (5)

8 Club of England left-back Stephen Warnock (5, 5)

9 England's speedy winger from Tottenham, Aaron _____ (6)

10 The number of lions England have on their badge (5)

MY SCORE... **OUT OF 100**

MY MATE'S...   MY DAD'S...

ROBIN VAN PERSIE!

Ten points for each right answer on the superstar!

1 How many goals did Robin score in Arsenal's 3-0 win against Tottenham this season?

A 0 **B** 1 **C** 2 ✓

2 How many games has Van Persie played for Holland?

A 0-20 ✓
B 30-50
C 60-80

3 In which year did he win his first cap for his country?

A 2004 ✓
B 2007
C 2010

4 How old is the Dutch striker?

A 26 **B** 31 **C** 36

5 Which footy boots does Van Persie wear?

A Adidas ✓
B Lotto
C Puma

6 What shirt number does Van Persie wear at Arsenal?

A 5 **B** 11 ✓ **C** 60

7 How many World Cups has he played in?

A 0 **B** 1 **C** 2

8 Which foot does Robin prefer to hit the ball with?

A Left ✓
B Right

9 Which of these did he achieve in the 2008-09 season?

A Got the most red cards
B Slid on his knees the most
C Set up the most Prem goals ✓

10 Arsenal signed Van Persie in 2004 from which club?

A Feyenoord ✓
B Real Madrid
C Yeovil

MY SCORE... **OUT OF 100**

 MY MATE'S...  MY DAD'S...

45

TEAM KIT CHALLENGE!

Four top World Cup stars need to find their kit before the match, but which of these routes will take them to the correct shirt? Get 25 points for each right answer!

1 Jermain Defoe ☐ 2 Gianluigi Buffon ☐ 3 Luis Fabiano ☐ 4 David Villa ☐

☐ MY SCORE... OUT OF 100

☐ MY MATE'S... ☐ MY DAD'S...

SQUAD SELECTION!

Tick the players who have been to previous World Cups and cross those who haven't – it's ten points for each!

1 DAVID JAMES
Been to a World Cup?

2 GLEN JOHNSON
Been to a World Cup?

3 OWEN HARGREAVES
Been to a World Cup?

4 JERMAINE JENAS
Been to a World Cup?

5 ASHLEY YOUNG
Been to a World Cup?

MY SCORE... **OUT OF 50**

MY MATE'S...   MY DAD'S...

47

DADS V LADS

Get your dad to answer the questions on the left while you do the right – ten points for each correct answer!

1986

1 Which team won the 1986 World Cup?

2 Which country hosted the 1986 World Cup?

3 Name one of England's three group opponents from this tournament!

4 Who was the England manager?

5 Who scored an amazing solo goal against England in the quarter-finals?

NOW

1 Who are the European champions going into this year's World Cup?

2 Which TV presenter hosts Match of the Day 2?

3 Name one of England's five opponents from their World Cup qualifying group!

4 How old is England boss Fabio Capello – 53 or 63?

5 Who was England's penalty-taker in their qualifying matches?

MY SCORE... **OUT OF 50** MY DAD'S...

49

MYSTERY MOBILE!

Which superstar owns this mobile phone? 50 points if you get it right!

WHAT U DOING FOR UR 33RD BIRTHDAY THIS SUMMER?

HOW'S CHELSEA? WEATHER MUST BE DIFFERENT TO BARCELONA!

GOOD LUCK AT THE WORLD CUP WITH PORTUGAL!

CAN U SHOW ME UR 2 CHAMPO LEAGUE WINNERS MEDALS SOMETIME?

I JUST GOT UR NAME AND 20 ON THE BACK OF MY BLUES SHIRT!

WHO IS IT?

MY SCORE...

OUT OF 50

MY MATE'S...

MY DAD'S...

50

TEAM SHEET!

Fill in the gaps and get ten points for each one!

2010 WORLD CUP GROUP A
FRANCE v MEXICO
THURSDAY 17 JUNE

FRANCE

Hugo LLORIS	GK	Lyon
Bacary	DF	Arsenal
.... GALLAS	DF	Arsenal
Eric ABIDAL	DF	Barcelona
Patrice	DF	Man. United
Lassana DIARRA	MF	Real ......
Alou DIARRA	MF	Bordeaux
Yoann GOURCUFF	MF	Bordeaux
Andre-Pierre GIGNAC	ST	Toulouse
Thierry ..... (C)	ST	....
.... ANELKA	ST	....

MEXICO

Guillermo OCHOA	GK	America
Rafael MARQUEZ (C)	DF	Barcelona
Jonny MAGALLON	DF	Guadalajara
Carlos SALCIDO	DF	PSV
Ricardo OSORIO	DF	Stuttgart
Israel CASTRO	MF	UNAM
Andres GUARDADO	MF	Deportivo
Gerardo TORRADO	MF	Cruz Azul
GIOVANI Dos Santos	MF	Tottenham
Miguel SABAH	ST	Morelia
Carlos VELA	ST	....

SUBSTITUTES

Steve MANDANDA, Julien ESCUDE, ... MALOUDA, Sidney GOVOU, Karim BENZEMA

SUBSTITUTES

Oswaldo SANCHEZ, Jose Antonio CASTRO, Pablo BARRERA, Francisco PALENCIA, Cuauhtemoc BLANCO

MANAGER Raymond DOMENECH   **MANAGER** Javier AGUIRRE

MY SCORE... OUT OF 100

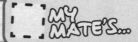
MY MATE'S...

MY DAD'S.

51

AARON LENNON!

Ten points for each right answer on the superstar!

1 Which of these trophies has Aaron Lennon already got his hands on?

A Carling Cup
B FA Cup ✓
C UEFA Cup

2 Is he left-footed or right-footed?

A Left
B Right ✓

3 In which big England qualifier was he named Man of the Match?

A Ukraine 1-0 England ✓
B England 5-1 Croatia
C England 2-1 Ukraine

4 Who is the youngest star – Aaron Lennon or Jermain Defoe?

A Lennon ✓
B Defoe

5 How many games has Aaron played for England?

A 10-20
B 30-40
C 50-60

6 Which footy boots does the speedster wear?

A Umbro
B Adidas ✓
C Nike ✓

7 Azza started his career at which club?

A Juventus
B LA Galaxy
C Leeds ✓

8 How old is Aaron Lennon?

A 23 B 27 C 31

9 How many World Cups has he been to with England?

A 0 ✓ B 1 C 2

10 What shirt number does he wear on his back at Tottenham?

A 10 B 7 ✓ C 14

MY SCORE... **OUT OF 100**

MY MATE'S...   MY DAD'S...

JOIN THE DOTS!

Link the dots together to reveal a key figure from a footy match!

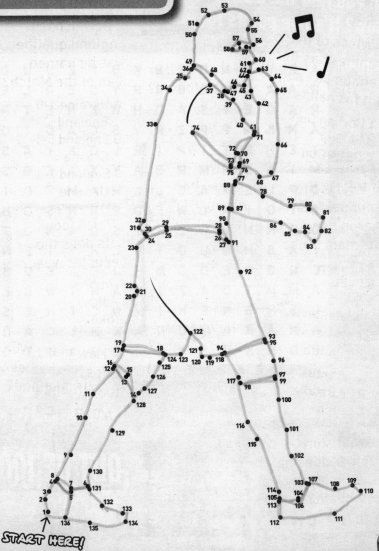

START HERE!

53

MEGA WORDSEARCH!

Can you find the 20 top midfielders that are hiding below? It's five points for each name you can find!

Alonso

Barry

Cahill

Deco

Dempsey

De Rossi

Diarra

Fabregas

Malouda

Mikel

Nakamura

Nani

Palacios

Park

Pienaar

A	R	V	A	N	D	E	R	K	B	F	E	J	U	D
R	A	A	D	M	B	B	B	R	P	Y	D	E	R	L	E
R	A	O	E	I	S	A	D	H	W	E	N	E	T	R
A	N	K	M	P	P	Z	R	V	S	C	A	G	I	O
I	E	H	P	T	I	P	I	R	L	O	K	I	A	S
M	I	A	S	R	M	R	B	A	Y	X	A	E	G	S
D	P	L	E	A	A	C	L	L	R	A	M	T	O	I
S	Y	O	Y	A	L	W	E	D	P	R	N	S	G	N
O	P	N	N	V	O	L	K	T	S	Q	A	N	D	T
I	A	S	H	R	U	O	I	V	L	H	Y	I	E	N
C	R	O	G	E	D	G	M	H	J	R	E	E	D	S
A	M	M	T	D	A	Z	I	N	A	N	I	W	B	E
L	S	N	S	N	E	K	I	M	W	C	T	H	E	S
A	N	A	K	A	M	U	R	A	K	N	L	C	A	Q
P	G	N	K	V	F	A	B	R	E	G	A	S	T	C

Pirlo

Schweinsteiger

Senna

Tiago

Van der Vaart

MY SCORE... OUT OF 100

MY MATE'S...

MY DAD'S...

54

COOL FINISHING!

Fit the right set of three letters into the correct word below – it's ten points for each right answer!

AND

ROP

PEN

TIM

ALF

ORT

NES

OFF

ICK

REE

1. F R E E - K _ _ _
2. _ _ _ A L T Y
3. F U L L - _ _ _ E
4. E N G L _ _ _
5. T _ _ _ _ H Y
6. _ _ _ S I D E
7. R E F E _ _ _
8. L I _ _ _ M A N
9. H _ _ _ T I M E
10. S U P P _ _ _ E R

MY SCORE... OUT OF 100

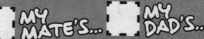

MY MATE'S... MY DAD'S...

55

NAME GAME!

Do you know these five players? Fill in the missing letters on their shirts – 20 points for each!

1 R_DRI_UE_ — 11 — ARGENTINA

2 _ERR_ — 15 — ENGLAND

3 HE_R_ — 12 — FRANCE

4 B__FO_ — 1 — ITALY

5 S_EIJ_E_ — 10 — HOLLAND

MY SCORE... **OUT OF 100**

MY MATE'S...

MY DAD'S...

DEFENSIVE DUOS!

DEFENSIVE DUOS!

Draw a line to link the defenders who play for the same country — it's 20 points for each right pair!

1 William **GALLAS**

2 LUCIO

3 Emmanuel **EBOUE**

4 Giorgio **CHIELLINI**

5 Carles **PUYOL**

KOLO TOURE

FABIO CANNAVARO

CARLOS MARCHENA

LUISAO

ERIC ABIDAL

MY SCORE...
OUT OF 100
MY MATE'S...
MY DAD'S...

57

CARLOS TEVEZ!

Ten points for each right answer on the superstar!

1 When did Carlos join Man. City?

A 2008
B 2009
C 2010 ✓

2 How many games has he played for Argentina?

A 0-10
B 20-40 ✓
C 50-60

3 Carlos scored his first hat-trick for Man. City against which Prem club?

A Blackburn ✓
B Man. United
C Arsenal

4 What shirt number does Tevez wear at Man. City?

A 10   B 23   C 32 ✓

5 What's his best position?

A Defender
B Midfielder
C Forward ✓

6 Tev introduced us to his unique goal celebration this season – what is it?

A A little dance ✓
B A somersault
C Digging up the penalty-spot

7 How many goals did he put past Man. United in the Carling Cup semi-finals?

A 1   B 3 ✓   C 7

8 Which trophy did Tevez NOT win at Man. United?

A Carling Cup
B FA Cup
C Champions League ✓

9 How old is he?

A 21   B 26 ✓   C 31

10 Which Prem club did Tev play for first?

A West Ham ✓
B Tottenham
C Sunderland

MY SCORE... **OUT OF 100**

MY MATE'S...

MY DAD'S...

58

LINK-U PLAY

Put a block from Group A next to a block from Group B to make a **World Cup** word. One's already been done for you – it's ten points for each pair you get right!

GROUP A

COR

WIN	GRE	REP	KEE
TOR	SER	DRO	CAH
MIL	GRO		

GROUP B

~~NER~~

RES	ILL	NER	UPS
BIA	GER	ECE	GBA
LAY	PER		

A	B
COR	NER

MY SCORE... **OUT OF 100**

MY MATE'S...

MY DAD'S...

59

WHOSE INBOX?

Guess which star is receiving these emails – 50 points if you get it right!

1

Subject: Quick message
From: Tony
Sent: May 2010

My missus says your wife, Alex, is writing some awesome columns in the Daily Mirror at the moment!

Thought I'd pass on the good vibe!

Tony

2

Subject: Liverpool legend!
From: Mr. Connor
Sent: May 2010

Dear Sir,

Thank you for signing my son's Liverpool No.8 shirt!

Kind regards,

Richard Connor

3

Subject: England star!
From: George Smith
Sent: May 2010

Hi mate, I'm so excited about the World Cup! How are you finding it on the left for England? At least it allows Lamps to play in the middle and you're linking up with Wazza well!

COME ON ENGLAND!
George

4

Subject: Stat of the week!
From: Statto
Sent: May 2010

Hey up, lad!

Here's my stat of the week. Did you know you've played over 350 games for Liverpool now? Amazing stuff! Keep it up!

Stat-Master-Flex!

WHO IS IT?

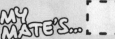

MY SCORE... OUT OF 50

MY MATE'S...   MY DAD'S...

PREM LINK!

Match these stars at the World Cup with their Prem clubs - ten points for each correct answer!

1 NICOLAS ANELKA
Country: FRANCE
Club:
....

2 ROBERT GREEN
Country: ENGLAND
Club:
....

3 ANDERSON
Country: BRAZIL
Club:
....

4 ANDRE BIKEY
Country: CAMEROON
Club:
....

5 CLINT DEMPSEY
Country: USA
Club:
....

6 DIRK KUYT
Country: HOLLAND
Club: Liverpool
....

7 MAYNOR FIGUEROA
Country: HONDURAS
Club: wigan
....

8 RYAN NELSEN
Country: NEW ZEALAND
Club: wesbrlyn
....

9 YAKUBU
Country: NIGERIA
Club: Blackburn
....

10 SAMIR NASRI
Country: FRANCE
Club: Arsenal
....

BURNLEY
WIGAN
LIVERPOOL
CHELSEA
WEST HAM
MAN. UNITED
EVERTON
ARSENAL
FULHAM
BLACKBURN

MY SCORE... **OUT OF 100**
MY MATE'S...
MY DAD'S...

61

10 QUESTIONS ON

Ten points for each correct answer!

1 What is the Dutch team's nickname?

- **A** Tulips
- **B** The Windmill Boys
- **C** Oranje

2 Which Prem star holds the record for being Holland's most-capped player ever?

- **A** Edwin van der Sar
- **B** Ryan Babel
- **C** Dirk Kuyt

3 Who's the Holland captain?

- **A** Giovanni van Bronckhorst
- **B** Mark van Bommel
- **C** Rafael van der Vaart

4 Midfielder Nigel de Jong plays for which Prem club?

- **A** Man. United
- **B** Man. City
- **C** Wigan

5 How many World Cup finals have Holland reached in their history?

A 2 **B** 1 **C** 0

TRUE OR FALSE?

Which facts are true and which are false? Get ten points for each correct answer!

1 This year's World Cup final will take place in Manchester!

True False

2 Sergio Aguero plays for Spain!

True False

3 David Beckham has played over 100 games for England!

True False

4 Nobody scored a hat-trick at the last World Cup!

True False

HOLLAND

6 Who's the Holland gaffer?

A Bertie Bassett
B Bert and Ernie
C Bert van Marwijk

7 Which star moved from Real Madrid to Inter Milan last summer?

A Wesley Sneijder
B Klaas-Jan Huntelaar
C Glenn Loovens

8 Which club does wicked winger Arjen Robben play for?

A Stuttgart
B Bayern Munich
C Hamburg

9 Which of these Dutch players is at Everton?

A Andre Ooijer
B John Heitinga
C Demy de Zeeuw

10 In which year did they win the Euro Championship?

A 1988
B 1996
C 2008

MY SCORE... OUT OF 100   MY MATE'S...   MY DAD'S...

5 The 2006 World Cup final was decided on a penalty shoot-out!

True False

6 Barcelona's Xavi plays for Chile!

True False

7 This year's World Cup football is made by Adidas!

True False

8 Chelsea midfielder John Obi Mikel is the Nigeria captain!

True False

9 Japan's home shirt is blue!

True False

10 There are roses on the England team badge!

True False

MY SCORE... OUT OF 100   MY MATE'S...   MY DAD'S...

CROSSWORD FUN!

Get ten points for each right answer!

DOWN

1 Inter Milan's Portuguese gaffer _____ Mourinho (4)

2 Chelsea centre-back Ricardo _____ (8)

4 Man. United's Portuguese winger (4)

5 Portugal centre-back Pepe plays for this club (4, 6)

6 Country that Portugal knocked out of the 2006 World Cup (7)

8 Colour of Portugal's home shirt (3)

ACROSS

3 Portuguese right-back Paulo Ferreira plays for this club (7)

7 Ronaldo's shirt number at Real Madrid (4)

9 Deco joined Chelsea from this club (9)

10 Big Portuguese club that won the Champions League in 2004 (5)

MY SCORE... **OUT OF 100**

MY MATE'S...   MY DAD'S...

64

ANSWERS ON PAGE 211 (DON'T CHEAT!)

WHO AM I?

Can you work out this star from these clues? 50 points if you're right!

WHO IS IT?

....

MY SCORE... OUT OF 50

MY MATE'S...

MY DAD'S...

JAMES MILNER!

Ten points for each right answer on the superstar!

1 Before joining Aston Villa, Milner played 100 games for which club?

- **A** Newcastle
- **B** Liverpool
- **C** Wolves

2 Who did he make his England debut against last year?

- **A** India
- **B** Holland
- **C** Jamaica

3 At which club did Milner start his professional career?

- **A** Nottingham Forest
- **B** Leeds
- **C** Sheff. Wednesday

4 How old is the Villa midfielder?

A 24 **B** 27 **C** 30

5 Milner has a nickname at Villa – but what is it?

- **A** J-Dog
- **B** Jilner
- **C** Milly

6 Which cup final did Milner score in this season?

- **A** Carling Cup final
- **B** Club World Cup final
- **C** UEFA Super Cup final

7 Milner has made a record number of appearances – but for which team?

- **A** England
- **B** England Under-21s
- **C** Aston Villa

8 In which season did Milner score the most goals?

- **A** 2007-08
- **B** 2008-09
- **C** 2009-10

9 Aston Villa paid a club record amount to buy Milner – but how much was it?

- **A** £12.5m
- **B** £6.5m
- **C** £20.5m

10 What shirt number does Milner have on his back at Villa?

A 8 **B** 9 **C** 10

MY SCORE... **OUT OF 100**

MY MATE'S... MY DAD'S...

66

JUMBLED UP!

Can you work out each of these World Cup countries? It's ten points for each one!

1 LATYI

2 ROIVY TOASC

3 ZILBRA

4 REBIAS

5 HANAG

6 GENTARINA

7 GERIALA

8 NODURASH

9 RALIASTAU

10 SLONEVIA

MY SCORE... **OUT OF 100**

MY MATE'S...

MY DAD'S...

67

WORLD CUP WINNERS!

Tick the stars who have won the World Cup or cross next to those who haven't – ten points for each!

1 GIANLUIGI BUFFON
Italy — ✓

2 KAKA
Brazil — ✗

3 DAVID BECKHAM
England — ✗

4 ALEXANDRE PATO
Brazil — ✗

5 PATRICK VIEIRA
France — ✓

6 CRISTIANO RONALDO
Portugal — ✗

7 DANIELE DE ROSSI
Italy — ✗

8 FRANCK RIBERY
France — ✗

9 ROBINHO
Brazil — ✗

10 LUCA TONI
Italy — ✓

MY SCORE... **OUT OF 100**

MY MATE'S...   MY DAD'S...

HIDDEN PLAYER!

Read the clues and write the four-lettered answers in the grid. They reveal the name of a player in the middle squares – it's 50 points if you know who it is!

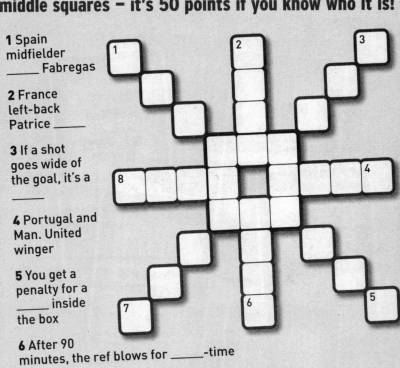

1 Spain midfielder _____ Fabregas

2 France left-back Patrice _____

3 If a shot goes wide of the goal, it's a _____

4 Portugal and Man. United winger

5 You get a penalty for a _____ inside the box

6 After 90 minutes, the ref blows for _____-time

7 Keepers can't touch the ball outside the penalty _____

8 Wembley holds 90,000 _____

WHO IS IT?
. . . .

MY SCORE... **OUT OF 50**

MY MATE'S...

MY DAD'S...

69

MYSTERY MOBILE!

Which top superstar owns this mobile phone? 50 points if you get it right!

BONJOUR WILL! GOOD LUCK MONSIEUR!

CONGRATS 4 SCORING ZE GOAL ZAT MADE FRANCE QUALIFY!

HOW COME UR A CENTRE-BACK BUT WEAR NO.10 4 UR CLUB?

U'LL B 1 OF MANY ARSENAL PLAYERS IN ZE FRANCE SQUAD!

GOOD LUCK FROM UR OLD MATE IN MARSEILLE!

WHO IS IT?
. . . .

MY SCORE...
OUT OF 50

MY MATE'S...

MY DAD'S...

DADS V LADS

Get your dad to answer the questions on the left while you do the right – ten points for each correct answer!

1994

1 England were not in the World Cup, but who was their manager that year?

2 Which teams played in the 1994 World Cup final?

3 In which city was the World Cup final held?

4 Who was the captain of Brazil in the 1994 final?

5 Which team knocked the Republic of Ireland out of the World Cup that year?

NOW

1 True or false – Fabio Capello is the first foreign manager that England have had!

2 Name one of the two European countries that won every single game in the World Cup qualifiers!

3 In which city will this year's World Cup final be held?

4 Who's the Spain captain that also plays for Real Madrid?

5 Who beat the Republic of Ireland in the World Cup qualifying play-offs?

MY DAD'S... OUT OF 50 MY SCORE...

QUALIFIED?

Put a tick next to the country if they made it to South Africa or a cross if they didn't – it's ten points for each!

1 CROATIA ✗

Did they qualify? ✗

2 ISRAEL ✡

Did they qualify? ✗

3 MEXICO

Did they qualify? ✓

4 SCOTLAND

Did they qualify? ✗

WHICH COUNTRY?

1 — E

2 — J

3 — F

4 — G

5 — D

6 — J

7 — B

8 — H

9 — C

10 — A

5 NEW ZEALAND
Did they qualify? ✓

6 PARAGUAY
Did they qualify? ✓

7 CANADA
Did they qualify? ✗

9 SERBIA
Did they qualify? ✗

10 SLOVENIA
Did they qualify? ✓

8 SWEDEN
Did they qualify? ✓

MY SCORE... OUT OF 100
MY MATE'S...
MY DAD'S...

Link the national flags to the country they belong to – ten points for each right answer!

A PORTUGAL   **F** SPAIN   **I** CHILE

B SOUTH KOREA   **G** NORTH KOREA

C SWITZERLAND   **H** JAPAN   **J** USA

D AUSTRALIA

E BRAZIL

MY SCORE... OUT OF 100
MY MATE'S...
MY DAD'S...

DAVID VILLA!

Ten points for each right answer on the superstar!

1 Which club has the Valencia striker NOT played for?

A Sporting Gijon
B Real Zaragoza
C Bayern Munich ✓

2 True or false – he has always had bright blond hair!

A True
B False ✓

3 Villa holds Spain's record for scoring the most goals in one year – how many is that?

A 9 B 12 C 15 ✓

4 Which of these tournaments was David Villa the top scorer in?

A Euro 2004
B 2006 World Cup
C Euro 2008 ✓

5 What shirt number does he wear at Valencia?

A 7 ✓ B 23 C 99

6 In which year did he join Valencia and receive his first Spain cap?

A 1995
B 2000
C 2005 ✓

7 Who is David Villa's main strike partner for Spain?

A Fernando Torres
B Mikel Arteta
C Raul

8 How did he celebrate goals at the start of the season, after his daughter was born?

A Throwing a nappy
B Sitting in a pram
C Sucking his thumb ✓

9 True or false – Villa scored more goals than Fernando Torres in qualifying!

A True ✓
B False

10 How old is the Spanish hitman?

A 22 B 28 C 34

MY SCORE... **OUT OF 100**

MY MATE'S...

MY DAD'S...

NAME GAME!

Do you know these five players? Fill in the missing letters on their shirts – 20 points for each kit!

HULK
21 1
BRAZIL

A. COLE
3 2
ENGLAND

SONG
6 3
CAMEROON

DE JONG
8 4
HOLLAND

NANI
17 5
PORTUGAL

MY SCORE... OUT OF 100
MY MATE'S...
MY DAD'S...

75

MEGA WORDSEARCH!

Can you find the 20 top defenders that are hiding below? It's five points for each name you can find!

Abidal

Agger

Cannavaro

Chiellini

Heinze

Heitinga

Juan

Kyrgiakos

Lahm

Maicon

Mokoena

Neill

Nelsen

Pepe

Puyol

Senderos

Terry

Toure

Vidic

Zanetti

X	B	H	E	T	G	L	F	Q	C	Y	A	R	A	L
S	E	N	D	E	R	O	S	N	O	Q	R	K	O	J
U	W	G	P	L	B	Y	M	R	E	P	K	I	M	P
H	B	K	D	A	G	A	A	A	L	L	E	Q	B	U
C	E	G	F	Q	B	V	G	T	I	S	S	P	J	Y
M	M	I	D	C	A	I	G	G	L	C	H	E	E	O
I	M	P	T	N	H	M	D	L	E	L	O	S	N	L
R	K	V	N	I	H	I	I	A	K	R	O	N	R	Z
J	U	A	N	A	N	E	E	C	L	K	Z	A	E	A
S	C	T	L	Z	N	G	T	L	A	N	N	Z	Y	N
V	T	X	O	Z	S	C	A	I	L	E	N	R	B	E
X	Y	E	R	U	I	Y	G	U	O	I	R	C	A	T
O	P	D	C	D	R	R	D	K	E	E	N	L	R	T
V	Z	J	I	G	Y	E	O	H	T	L	E	I	R	I
W	L	V	Z	K	T	M	Y	F	Y	T	W	Q	G	U

MY SCORE... OUT OF 100

MY MATE'S...

MY DAD'S...

IN SQUAD OUT?
SELECTION!
IN? OUT?

Put a tick by the England stars if they have been to previous World Cups or a cross if they haven't – it's ten points for each correct answer!

1 PAUL ROBINSON
Were they selected?

2 SOL CAMPBELL
Were they selected?

3 JOLEON LESCOTT
Were they selected?

5 DARREN BENT
Were they selected?

4 DAVID BECKHAM
Were they selected?

MY SCORE... OUT OF 50

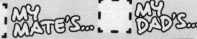

MY MATE'S... MY DAD'S...

77

WHO AM I?

Can you name this top star from their clues? 50 points if you're right!

I was the second-youngest member of France's Euro 2008 squad!

I wear number eight for my club!

Our fans call me Sammy!

I joined Arsenal from Marseille in 2008!

I scored four minutes into my Gunners debut against West Brom!

I broke my leg last summer!

I'm right-footed!

I'm a 22 year-old versatile midfielder!

WHO IS IT?

....

MY SCORE... OUT OF 50

MY MATE'S...

MY DAD'S...

10 QUESTIONS ON FRANCE

Ten points for each correct answer!

1 What is the nickname of the French team?

A Les Bleus
B Eau de Toilette
C Deja vu

2 Right-back Bacary Sagna plays for which Prem side?

A Arsenal
B Chelsea
C Tottenham

3 At which top stadium do they play their home matches?

A Le Cafe Stadium
B Stade de France
C Fromage Frais Stade

4 Which star is the all-time top scorer for France?

A Younes Kaboul
B Karim Benzema
C Thierry Henry

5 Their home kit is blue, but what colour is the away kit?

A Purple
B Green
C White

6 Ex-Porstmouth midfielder Lassana Diarra now plays for which club?

A Bayern Munich
B Real Madrid
C Barcelona

7 Which animal have France got on their badge?

A Meerkat
B Cockerel
C Hippopotamus

8 Which of these three stars have the most caps?

A William Gallas
B Hatem Ben Arfa
C Yoann Gourcuff

9 How many times have France won the World Cup?

A 0   B 1   C 5

10 Who's the boss?

A Michel Platini
B Arsene Wenger
C Raymond Domenech

MY SCORE... **OUT OF 100**

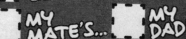

MY MATE'S...   MY DAD'S...

79

WHOSE INBOX?

Guess which star is receiving these emails – 50 points if you get it right!

1

Subject: Lucky 13!
From: Jurgen Flurgun
Sent: April 2010

You know that you wear number 13 for club and country? Well, Germany's first game at the World Cup is on 13 June – maybe it's a lucky sign!

Best wishes,
Jurgen

2

Subject: Re: Last World Cup?
From: Karl-Heinz Rumourmonger
Sent: April 2010

Hey man,

Good luck in your third World Cup! Do you think it'll be your last one now that you're 33 years old?

Cheers
KH

3

Subject: ‹No subject›
From: Franz Pantz
Sent: May 2010

Hey Mike,

When are you leaving London to go to the World Cup in South Africa?

From
Franz

4

Subject: Re: 2010 World Cup
From: Rudi Poody
Sent: May 2010

You're right, it's going to be a great tournament!
Hopefully you'll captain Germany to success and add to your tally of over 40 goals for them.

Regards,
Rudi

WHO IS IT?

@

MY SCORE... **OUT OF 50**

MY MATE'S...

MY DAD'S...

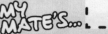

SHADY PIC!

Shade in each fragment containing two dots to reveal a footy picture!

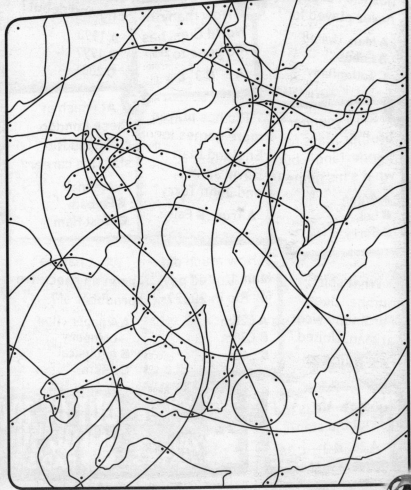

RIO FERDINAND!

Ten points for each right answer on the superstar!

1 Which of these clubs has Rio Ferdinand never played for?

A Man. United
B Leeds
C Tottenham

2 How many World Cups has Rio gone to?

A 0 B 3 C 6

3 In which year did he make his England debut?

A 1993
B 1997
C 2001

4 Rio's younger brother plays for Sunderland – but what's his name?

A Anton
B Les
C Barry

5 Rio has played more games for England than David James and John Terry?

A True B False

6 At which of these London clubs did Rio start his career?

A Arsenal
B Fulham
C West Ham

7 What shirt number does Ferdinand wear at Man. United?

A 5 B 10 C 23

8 How much did Man. United pay for Rio in 2002?

A £20m
B £30m
C £40m

9 What has he been an executive producer of?

A A paper clip company
B A musical
C A film

10 How old is the England star?

A 26 B 31 C 36

 MY SCORE... **OUT OF 100**

 MY MATE'S...   MY DAD'S...

ANSWERS ON PAGE 214 (DON'T CHEAT!)

SIL-WHO-ETTE!

Can you name these MOTD experts?
25 points for each right answer!

WHO IS IT?

1...............

WHO IS IT?

2...............

MY SCORE... OUT OF 50

MY MATE'S...

MY DAD'S...

TEAM SHEET!

Fill in the gaps and get ten points for each one!

2010 WORLD CUP GROUP E
CAMEROON v HOLLAND
THURSDAY 24 JUNE

CAMEROON

Carlos KAMENI	GK	Espanyol
Benoit ASSOU-EKOTTO	DF	....
Nicolas N'KOULOU	DF	Monaco
Aurelien CHEDJOU	DF	Lille
GEREMI	DF	Ankaragucu
.... SONG	MF	Arsenal
Jean MAKOUN	MF	Lyon
Georges MANDJECK	MF	K'slautern
Achille EMANA	MF	Real Betis
...... ETO'O (C)	ST	Inter .....
Mohamadou IDRISSOU	ST	Freiburg

HOLLAND

Maarten STEKELENBURG	GK	Ajax
John HEITINGA	DF	Everton
Andre OOIJER	DF	PSV
Joris MATHIJSEN	DF	Hamburg
Gio VAN BRONCKHORST (C)	DF	Feyenoord
Nigel DE JONG	MF	... .
Mark VAN BOMMEL	MF	Bayern Munich
Wesley SNEIJDER	MF	..... Milan
Dirk	ST	Liverpool
Arjen ROBBEN	ST	....
Robin ... PERSIE	ST	....

SUBSTITUTES

Souleymanou HAMIDOU,
Henri BEDIMO, Stephane M'BIA,
Eyong ENOH, Pierre WEBO

SUBSTITUTES

Michel VORM, Khalid BOULAHROUZ,
Ryan BABEL, Rafael VAN DER VAART,
Klaas-Jan HUNTELAAR

MANAGER   Paul LE GUEN

MANAGER   Bert VAN MARWIJK

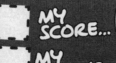

MY SCORE... **OUT OF 100**

MY MATE'S...

MY DAD'S...

CROSSWORD FUN!

Get ten points for each right answer!

DOWN

1 Slovenia captain Robert Koren played in the Championship this season for West _____ (4)

2 USA and Fulham winger _____ Dempsey (5)

3 Colour of Mexico's home shirt (5)

4 Uruguay star striker Diego Forlan plays for _____ Madrid (8)

6 Liverpool defender Sotirios Kyrgiakos plays for this country (6)

8 Colour of Denmark's home shirt (3)

ACROSS

5 Man. United's Park Ji-Sung plays for _____ Korea (5)

7 Australia star Tim Cahill plays for this club (7)

9 Switzerland and West Ham midfielder Valon _____ (7)

10 Country that Liverpool's centre-back Martin Skrtel plays for (8)

MY SCORE... **OUT OF 100**

MY MATE'S...   MY DAD'S...

85

TRUE OR FALSE?

Which facts are true and which are false? Circle the right answers – get ten points for each one!

1 England won the World Cup back in 1966!

True False

2 Nigeria's nickname is the Super Eagles!

True False

3 Tottenham superstar Luka Modric plays for South Korea!

True False

4 The name of this year's World Cup mascot is Zakumi!

True False

5 Portsmouth's Aaron Mokoena is the South Africa captain!

True False

6 England's footy shirts are made by Umbro!

True False

7 Man. United winger Antonio Valencia plays for Portugal!

True False

8 Sven-Goran Eriksson is the manager of Denmark!

True False

9 Aaron Lennon played in the last World Cup!

True False

10 Arsenal left-back Gael Clichy plays for France!

True False

MY SCORE... **OUT OF 100**

MY MATE'S...

MY DAD'S...

NAME GAME!

Can you identifty these stars? Fill in the missing letters on their shirts – 20 points for each kit!

_ERDI_AN_
5 **1**
ENGLAND

_AHM
16 **2**
GERMANY

E__IE_
8 **3**
GHANA

_UY_
9 **4**
HOLLAND

_ASI_LA_
1 **5**
SPAIN

MY SCORE... OUT OF 100

MY MATE'S...

MY DAD'S...

87

COOL FINISHING!

Fit the right set of three letters into the correct word below – it's ten points for each right answer!

RAN

MAN

TUG

SPA

ERB

AND

TIN

AZI

EXI

ALY

1. P O R _ _ _ A L
2. B R _ _ _ L
3. F _ _ _ C E
4. I T
5. A R G E N _ _ _ A
6. H O L L _ _ _
7. _ _ _ I N
8. M _ _ _ C O
9. S _ _ _ I A
10. G E R _ _ _ Y

MY SCORE... OUT OF 100

MY MATE'S...

MY DAD'S...

89

KAKA!

Ten points for each right answer on the superstar!

1 The wicked Brazil playmaker joined Real Madrid last year from which club?

A AC Milan
B Bayern Munich
C Inter Milan

2 Which Prem club came close to buying Kaka last year?

A Man. City
B Arsenal
C Liverpool

3 How many caps has he won for the Brazil team?

A 30-40
B 50-60
C 70-80

4 Kaka was in the Brazil squad that won the World Cup in which year?

A 2006
B 2002
C 1998

5 In which year was he named the World Player of the Year?

A 2005
B 2007
C 2009

6 Kaka was once named Player of the Tournament – but for which competition?

A 2009 Confederations Cup
B 2007 Copa America
C 2006 World Cup

7 Kaka's full name is:

A Ricardo Izecson dos Santos Leite
B Super Cali Fragilistic Expialidocious
C Keith Robert Samuel Sanchez

8 How does Kaka celebrate every time he scores?

A He somersaults
B Slides along the grass on his knees
C Points to the sky

9 What shirt number does Kaka wear at Real Madrid?

A 4 B 6 C 8

10 How old is he?

A 24 B 28 C 32

MY SCORE... **OUT OF 100**

MY MATE'S... MY DAD'S...

MYSTERY MOBILE!

Which World Cup star owns this mobile phone? It's 50 points if you get it right!

DON'T FORGET TO TAKE UR NIKE BOOTS WITH U!

HEY BLONDIE! SCORE SOME GOALS 4 ME!

YO EL NINO! U GOT ANY SPARE SPAIN TICKETS?

YOU GETTING ANY MORE TATTOOS ON UR ARMS?

GOOD LUCK WIV SPAIN. C U AT LIV NXT SEASON!

WHO IS IT?

. . . .

MY SCORE...

OUT OF 50

MY MATE'S...

MY DAD'S...

TRUE OR FALSE?

Which facts are true and which are false? Circle the right answers — it's ten points for each one!

1 Italy's national anthem was produced by Kanye West!

True False

2 Brazil won the 2006 World Cup!

True False

3 Holland's nickname is The Blues!

True False

4 Patrick Vieira has played over 100 games for France!

True False

5 Man. United keeper Edwin van der Sar has retired from international football!

True False

6 Tottenham midfielder Wilson Palacios plays for Honduras!

True False

7 USA, Algeria and Slovenia are in England's World Cup group!

True False

8 Chelsea's ace midfielder Florent Malouda plays for France!

True False

9 Cesc Fabregas is captain of the Spain team!

True False

10 Top Man. City keeper Shay Given plays for Slovenia!

True False

MY SCORE... **OUT OF 100**

MY MATE'S...

MY DAD'S...

LINK-U PLAY

Put a block from Group A next to a block from Group B to make a **World Cup** word. One's already been done for you — it's ten points for each pair you get right!

GROUP B BLEY

ENCE	LAND	MANY	IKER
ALTY	MARK	EREE	GUAY
ERIA	STLE

GROUP A WEM

GER	PEN	DEN	REF
HOL	WHI	ALG	DEF
URU	STR

| A | B |
| WEM | BLEY |

MY SCORE... **OUT OF 100**

MY MATE'S...

MY DAD'S...

93

HIDDEN TEAM!

Read the clues and write the four-lettered answers in the grid. They reveal the name of a team in the middle squares – it's 50 points if you can name it!

1 France and Barcelona left-back _____ Abidal

2 Aaron Lennon's nickname _____

3 Players go back to their changing _____ at half-time

4 Liverpool's Spanish keeper _____ Reina

5 England have a _____ directly above their badge to show they've won a World Cup

6 Arsenal's English speedster _____ Walcott

7 Ivory Coast and Man. City centre-back _____ Toure

8 England and Liverpool right-back _____ Johnson

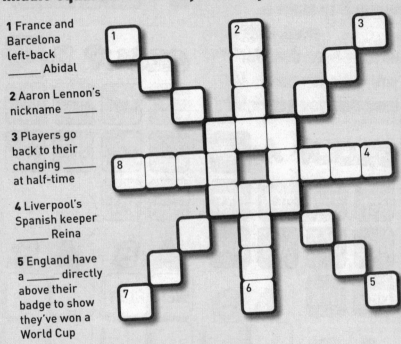

TEAM NAME:

MY SCORE... OUT OF 50

MY MATE'S...

MY DAD'S...

94

WHO AM I?

Guess who this star is from these clues — get 50 points if you're right!

I joined Man. United from Sporting Lisbon in 2007!

I'm a skilful winger, with bags of speed!

I love bright-coloured football boots, like yellow!

This will be my first World Cup, but I was at Euro 2008!

I like to celebrate my goals by doing a somersault!

I love to shoot from far out!

I'm just 23 years old!

My shirt number is 17 for my club!

WHO IS IT?

. . . .

MY SCORE... **OUT OF 50**

MY MATE'S...

MY DAD'S...

95

FRANK LAMPARD!

1 On which of these computer games can Frank be seen on the cover?

A FIFA 10
B PES 2010
C Mario Strikers Charged Football

2 What colour footy boots hasn't he worn this season in the Prem?

A Gold
B Pink
C White

3 What is Lampard's nickname?

A Lampshade
B Lamps
C Frankster

5 In which year did Frank make his England debut?

A 1999
B 2003
C 2007

4 What number does he have on the back of his Chelsea shirt?

A 10   B 9   C 8

MY SCORE...

RAPPING ROWS!

1 If you're fouled, you get a _____-kick
2 Match of the Day expert _____ Dixon
3 The name of England's 90,000-seater stadium

4 Chelsea and England left-back Ashley _____
5 When the ball hits the net, it's a _____!
6 West Ham and England striker Carlton _____

1	2	3
4	5	6
7	8	9
10	11	12

It's ten points each for each right answer on the midfield magician!

6 At which club did Lampard start his career?

A Fulham
B West Ham
C Tottenham

7 Which of these games did Frank score in?

A 2009 Champions League final
B Euro 2008 final
C 2008 Champions League final

8 How old will he be when the World Cup starts?

A 31 B 33 C 35

9 How many World Cups has he played in before this year?

A 0 B 1 C 2

10 How many goals did he score in England's 5-1 win against Croatia in qualifying?

A 1 B 2 C 3

OUT OF 100 ☐ MY MATE'S... ☐ MY DAD'S...

Write the answers to the clues in the spaces below – they all rhyme. Grab 25 points for each group!

7 Diego Forlan plays for this country
8 What did Rooney call his first son last year?
9 Roque Santa Cruz helped this country qualify

10 England are in World Cup Group ___
11 Surname of England's top scorer during qualifying
12 Country that Michael Ballack plays for

☐ MY SCORE... **OUT OF 100**
☐ MY MATE'S... ☐ MY DAD'S...

MEGA WORDSEARCH!

Can you find the 20 World Cup stars that are hiding below? It's five points for each name you can find!

Ballack
Buffon
Drogba
Essien
Eto'o
Gerrard
Iniesta
Kaka
Lampard
Messi
Ribery
Robinho
Ronaldo
Rooney
Sneijder

S	E	W	J	V	W	I	L	R	O	O	N	E	Y	Z
N	P	Q	K	K	A	O	N	A	M	O	C	Q	V	Z
E	L	M	T	E	H	N	B	A	M	E	T	V	U	V
I	S	G	F	N	B	G	P	G	Z	P	S	V	E	R
J	B	S	I	D	O	A	U	E	U	S	A	S	G	R
D	L	B	I	R	A	I	L	D	R	D	I	R	I	O
E	O	Z	D	E	X	I	N	L	U	S	Y	B	D	N
R	Q	B	I	J	N	O	D	I	A	R	I	X	Y	A
Q	V	A	B	Q	O	R	D	T	E	C	S	E	H	L
T	I	T	X	T	A	N	C	B	O	S	K	V	S	D
E	L	D	E	R	O	G	I	P	I	O	T	E	S	O
V	L	G	R	F	P	R	G	V	T	Y	R	A	I	D
E	A	E	F	Q	P	K	A	K	A	R	H	W	U	A
Z	G	U	F	E	G	X	L	I	O	M	Q	F	I	E
T	B	U	H	J	G	P	T	T	Y	T	P	B	T	L

Tevez

Torres

Van Persie

Villa

Xavi

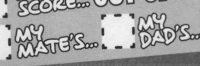

MY SCORE... OUT OF 100
MY MATE'S... MY DAD'S...

Circle the odd one out in each of the boxes below – get 20 points for each correct answer!

1
FERNANDO TORRES   GLEN JOHNSON
DIRK KUYT   WAYNE ROONEY

2
IKER CASILLAS   NICKLAS BENDTNER
MARK SCHWARZER   TIM HOWARD

3
DENMARK   SWITZERLAND
GHANA   ENGLAND

4
HOLLAND   FRANCE
ITALY   GERMANY

5
MEXICO   CAMEROON
ITALY   NIGERIA

MY SCORE... **OUT OF 100**
MY MATE'S...   MY DAD'S...

99

10 QUESTIONS ON ARGENTINA

Ten points for each correct answer!

1 Who is the Argentina captain?

A Javier Mascherano
B Gabriel Heinze
C Fabricio Coloccini

2 Which Prem club does young Argentina left-back Emiliano Insua play for?

A Liverpool
B Sunderland
C Everton

3 Which Argentina legend is currently their manager?

A Gabriel Batistuta
B Diego Maradona
C Hernan Crespo

4 Argentina winger Jonas Gutierrez plays for which club?

A West Brom
B Newcastle
C Nottingham Forest

5 Which Argentina star moved from Man. United to Man. City?

A Sylvinho
B Pablo Zabaleta
C Carlos Tevez

6 Which star holds the record for playing the most games for Argentina?

A Javier Zanetti
B Maxi Rodriguez
C Gonzalo Higuain

7 What letters are on the Argentina football badge?

A FA
B MLS
C AFA

8 What colour is their away shirt?

A White
B Blue
C Yellow

9 How many times have Argentina won the Copa America?

A 2 B 8 C 14

10 How many times have Argentina won the World Cup?

A 1 B 2 C 3

MY SCORE... **OUT OF 100**

MY MATE'S... MY DAD'S...

WHOSE INBOX?

Guess which star is receiving these emails – 50 points if you get it right!

1

Subject: ‹No subject›
From: Sergei
Sent: May 2010

Greetings Mate-ski,

Good luck in World Cup football games for Serbia, yes? I be cheering for you in that nastski Group of Death!

Bye
Sergei

2

Subject: 29 in October!
From: Aleksandr
Sent: May 2010

Hey Vida,

I invited all of your old mates from Spartak Moscow over for your 29th birthday in October! It's going to be mint!

Best,
Aleks

3

Subject: Manchester
From: Tomislav
Sent: May 2010

Yo No.5!

I'm in Manchester next weekend. Can you recommend a good cafe? You must know the city well because it's where your club is!

Cheers,
Tom

4

Subject: Centre-back!
From: Rajko
Sent: May 2010

Wassup, big man?

After the World Cup, can you give my son some tips on how to become a no-nonsense centre-back, like yourself? He really wants to be a defender!

Thanks, you're a star! Rajko

WHO IS IT?

....

MY SCORE... **OUT OF 50**

MY MATE'S...

MY DAD'S...

JOIN THE DOTS!

Link the dots together to reveal a key figure from a footy match!

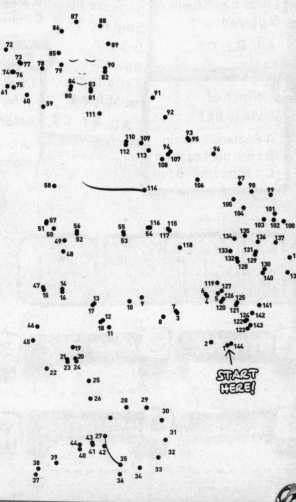

START HERE!

STEVEN GERRARD!

3 Which football boots does he wear?

A Adidas
B Nike
C Puma

2 How many goals did he score in England's 5-1 win against Croatia in qualifying?

A 0 **B** 1 **C** 2

1 How many clubs has Stevie G played for?

A 1 **B** 2 **C** 3

5 How many World Cups has he played in for England before this year?

A 0 **B** 1 **C** 2

4 Which of these is he?

A England captain
B Liverpool captain
C A Man. United fan

MY SCORE...

JUMBLED UP!

1 ROONMACE

2 RITZLANDSWE

3 DANHOLL

7 MARKNED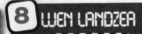

8 WEN LANDZEA

9 GUAYPARA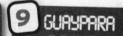

Pick up ten points for each right answer on the England star!

6 Stevie G is married, but what is his wife's name?

- **A** Alex
- **B** Lisa
- **C** Toni

7 Which of these games has he scored a goal in?

- **A** World Cup final
- **B** Champions League final
- **C** European Championship final

8 Stevie G was England's top scorer at which of these tournaments?

- **A** Euro 2004
- **B** 2006 World Cup
- **C** Euro 2008

9 What shirt number does he wear for Liverpool?

A 8 **B** 9 **C** 10

10 How old is Steven Gerrard?

A 29 **B** 33 **C** 37

OUT OF 100 ☐ **MY MATE'S...** ☐ **MY DAD'S...**

Can you work out who these World Cup countries are? It's ten points for each one!

4 HOUST FRACIA

5 RIAGIEN

6 NAISP

10 THOUS REAKO

☐ **MY SCORE...** **OUT OF 100**

☐ **MY MATE'S...** ☐ **MY DAD'S...**

CROSSWORD FUN!

It's ten points for each answer you get right on the Spain team!

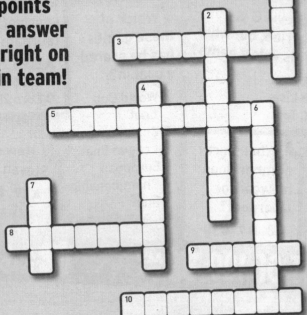

DOWN

1 Real Madrid striker and Spain's top scorer of all time (4)

2 Club that amazing midfielder Xavi plays for _____ (9)

4 The Spain captain is Iker _____ (8)

6 Xabi Alonso left this Prem club to join Real Madrid last year (9)

7 Shirt number that Fernando Torres wears at Liverpool (4)

ACROSS

3 Spain sometimes play home games at the Santiago _____ (8)

5 Spanish club that midfielder Marcos Senna plays for (10)

8 Spain and Barcelona midfielder Andres _____ (7)

9 Spain's long-haired right-back Sergio _____ (5)

10 Position that Cesc Fabregas plays in (8)

MY SCORE... OUT OF 100

MY MATE'S...   MY DAD'S...

WHO AM I?

Work out who this player is from the clues – it's 50 points if you're right!

I played for Crystal Palace on loan in the 1999-2000 season!

I'm a left-back who loves to bomb forward!

I've played for the losing side in two Champions League finals!

I want to reach 100 caps for England and I'm getting closer!

I played in the 2002 and 2006 World Cup!

I won three FA Cups and two Prems!

I won the Chelsea Players' Player of the Year award in 2009!

I'm 29 years old!

WHO IS IT?

....

MY SCORE... **OUT OF 50**

MY MATE'S...

MY DAD'S...

MIDFIELD MAESTROS!

MIDFIELD MAESTROS!

Draw a line to link the midfield partners of these countries – pick up 20 points for each right pair!

1 Thomas HITZLSPERGER

2 John Obi MIKEL

3 Daniele DE ROSSI

4 Nigel DE JONG

5 Lassana DIARRA

DICKSON ETUHU

MICHAEL BALLACK

WESLEY SNEIJDER

YOANN GOURCUFF

ANDREA PIRLO

MY SCORE...

OUT OF 100

MY MATE'S...

MY DAD'S...

HIDDEN COUNTRY!

Read the clues and write the four-lettered answers in the grid. They reveal the name of a country in the middle squares – it's 50 points if you can name it!

1 Fans do this when they slam their hands together

2 Portugal and Chelsea midfielder

3 Spain captain _____ Casillas

4 Holland and Liverpool star Dirk _____

5 Portsmouth's old Nigerian forward

6 England have the cross of St George on their _____

7 Real Madrid's Brazilian superstar midfielder

8 The World Cup _____ is made by Adidas and called Jabulani

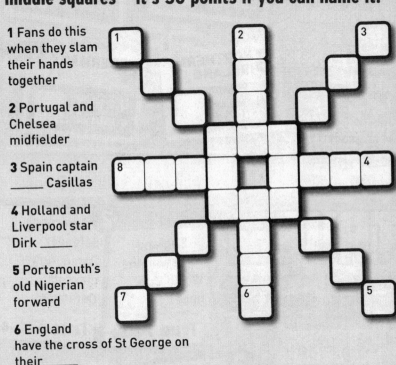

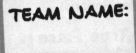

MY SCORE... **OUT OF 50**

MY MATE'S...

MY DAD'S...

109

QUALIFIED?

Put a tick next to the country if they made it to South Africa or a cross if they didn't – it's ten points for each!

1 ALGERIA
Did they qualify?

2 LATVIA
Did they qualify?

3 NORTHERN IRELAND
Did they qualify?

4 GERMANY
Did they qualify?

TRUE OR FALSE?

Which facts are true and which are false? Get ten points for each correct answer!

1 England have won the World Cup once!
True False

2 Liverpool defender Daniel Agger plays for Denmark!
True False

3 Newcastle winger Jonas Gutierrez plays for Argentina!
True False

4 Man. City powerhouse Emmanuel Adebayor plays for Holland!
True False

5 AUSTRIA

Did they qualify?

6 NORTH KOREA

Did they qualify?

7 ECUADOR

Did they qualify?

9 ITALY

Did they qualify?

10 ARGENTINA

Did they qualify?

8 BOSNIA & HERZEGOVINA

Did they qualify?

MY SCORE... OUT OF 100

MY MATE'S...

MY DAD'S...

5 Steven Gerrard is the captain of the USA!

True False

6 Theo Walcott was 17 when he went to the last World Cup with England!

True False

7 Germany, Australia, Serbia and Ghana are in the same group!

True False

8 Everton's tough midfielder Marouane Fellaini plays for Mexico!

True False

9 Portugal's home shirt is black!

True False

10 Chelsea defender Alex plays for Brazil!

True False

MY SCORE... OUT OF 100

MY MATE'S...

MY DAD'S...

MYSTERY MOBILE!

Which superstar owns this mobile phone? 50 points if you get it right!

YO! NO.3! GOOD LUCK WITH FRANCE IN SOUTH AFRICA DUDE!

HAPPY 29TH B'DAY FOR THE 15 MAY!

U MIGHT SEE UR TEAM-MATES RIO AND WAZZA OUT THERE!

HEY FRENCH BOY, WHEN U BACK IN MANCHESTER?

IF U MISS THE PLANE, U'LL B LEFT-BACK IN MORE THAN ONE WAY!

WHO IS IT?

. . . .

MY SCORE...

OUT OF 50

MY MATE'S...

MY DAD'S...

THIERRY HENRY!

Ten points for each right answer on the superstar!

1 The Barcelona hitman has played 254 games for which of these top clubs?

- **A** Stuttgart
- **B** Arsenal
- **C** Inter Milan

2 Which footy boots does Thierry wear?

- **A** Puma
- **B** Lotto
- **C** Reebok

3 Which of these clubs has he never played for?

- **A** Juventus
- **B** Monaco
- **C** Chelsea

4 What shirt number does Thierry wear?

- **A** 14 **B** 23 **C** 50

5 How old is the Frenchman?

- **A** 32 **B** 35 **C** 38

6 How many times has Thierry has been French Player of the Year?

- **A** 1 **B** 5 **C** 9

7 How many times has he won the World Cup?

- **A** 0 **B** 1 **C** 2

8 Henry has been the Prem's top scorer, but in how many seasons?

- **A** 0 **B** 2 **C** 4

9 How many times has Thierry won the European Championship?

- **A** 1 **B** 2 **C** 3

10 Which one of these players has never been his strike partner?

- **A** Robin van Persie
- **B** Emmanuel Adebayor
- **C** Jermain Defoe

MY SCORE... **OUT OF 100**

 MY MATE'S... MY DAD'S...

DADS V LADS

Get your dad to answer the questions on the left while you do the right – ten points for each correct answer!

1990

1. True or false – 1990 was the first time Italy had hosted the World Cup?

2. Which country lost in the final that year?

3. Which player won the Golden Boot?

4. Where did England finish – third or fourth?

5. How far did Scotland go in the tournament?

NOW

1. True or false? This is the first time South Africa has hosted a World Cup.

2. Who lost to Italy in the 2006 World Cup final?

3. How many goals did Wayne Rooney score in qualifying – five or nine?

4. Did England finish first or second in their qualifying group?

5. Name another country from Scotland's World Cup qualifying group!

MY SCORE...OUT OF 50 MY DAD'S...

SUPER STRIKERS!

SUPER STRIKERS!

Draw a line to link the team-mates who star for the same country – it's 20 points for a right pair!

1 Carlos **TEVEZ**

2 ROBINHO

3 Nicklas **BENDTNER**

4 Thierry **HENRY**

5 Fernando **TORRES**

DAVID VILLA

GONZALO HIGUAIN

NICOLAS ANELKA

JON DAHL TOMASSON

LUIS FABIANO

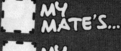

MY SCORE...

OUT OF 100

MY MATE'S...

MY DAD'S...

10 QUESTIONS ON
Ten points for each correct answer!

1 Which star is the Portugal captain?
- **A** Cristiano Ronaldo
- **B** Carles Puyol
- **C** Didier Drogba

2 Portugal reached the final of which tournament?
- **A** Euro 2004
- **B** 2007 Copa America
- **C** 2006 World Cup

3 Who is the Portugal gaffer?
- **A** Carlos Queiroz
- **B** Fabio Capello
- **C** Martin O'Neill

4 Which ex-Chelsea boss led Portugal at the 2006 World Cup?
- **A** Guus Hiddink
- **B** Avram Grant
- **C** Luiz Felipe Scolari

5 What colour is Portugal's away shirt?
- **A** Pink
- **B** White
- **C** Yellow

MY SCORE...

COUNTRY CONNECT!

Match the countries -

1 YAYA TOURE

2 KARIM BENZEMA

3 PHILIPP LAHM

4 ARJEN ROBBEN

5 ROBINHO

6 SERGIO AGUERO

7 WAYNE ROONEY

8 IKER CASILLAS

9 DANIELE DE ROSSI

10 BRANISLAV IVANOVIC

PORTUGAL!

6 Portugal's ace midfielder Miguel Veloso plays for which club?

A Man. United
B Sporting Lisbon
C Barcelona

7 What's Deco going to do after the World Cup finishes?

A Become a referee
B Form his own country
C Retire from international football

8 Right-back Jose Bosingwa plays for which Prem club?

A Liverpool
B Chelsea
C Arsenal

9 How old is Cristiano Ronaldo?

A 25 **B** 30 **C** 35

10 Attacking midfielder Danny plays for which Russian club?

A Zenit St. Borisburg
B Zenit St. Petersburg
C Zenit St. Adamburg

OUT OF 100 ☐ **MY MATE'S...** ☐ **MY DAD'S...**

World Cup stars with their World Cup
t's ten points for each correct answer!

A SPAIN **B** SERBIA **C** IVORY COAST

D ARGENTINA **E** GERMANY

F FRANCE **G** ENGLAND **H** BRAZIL

I ITALY

J HOLLAND

☐ **MY SCORE...** **OUT OF 100**

☐ **MY MATE'S...** ☐ **MY DAD'S...**

117

MEGA WORDSEARCH!

Can you find the 20 World Cup qualifiers hiding below? It's five points for each one you can find!

Algeria

Australia

Cameroon

Chile

Denmark

Ghana

Greece

Honduras

Japan

Mexico

New Zealand

North Korea

Paraguay

Serbia

Slovakia

S	O	U	T	H	A	F	R	I	C	A	J	Y	P	L
S	W	I	T	Z	E	R	L	A	N	D	N	E	I	G
H	M	C	K	E	U	A	A	F	Q	T	O	N	S	H
J	O	P	R	J	M	L	S	Z	B	X	R	E	L	A
A	C	N	U	R	U	G	U	A	Y	W	T	W	O	N
P	U	C	D	V	V	E	C	W	Y	E	H	Z	V	A
A	I	S	A	U	C	R	Q	H	C	Y	K	E	A	P
N	F	D	T	M	R	I	V	E	I	I	O	A	K	A
A	Y	E	R	R	E	A	E	O	Y	L	R	L	I	R
E	M	N	D	X	A	R	S	P	X	C	E	A	A	A
B	Z	M	U	T	G	L	O	Q	Q	G	A	N	T	G
O	I	A	J	S	B	B	I	O	S	J	D	D	C	U
S	E	R	B	I	A	J	A	A	N	C	H	V	X	A
R	R	K	V	M	F	A	M	E	X	I	C	O	I	Y
B	S	Y	K	S	L	O	V	E	N	I	A	Q	C	F

Slovenia

South Africa

Switzerland

Uruguay

USA

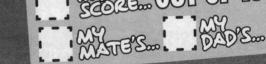

MY SCORE... OUT OF 100

MY MATE'S...

MY DAD'S...

DEBUT DELIGHT!

Match these players to the year that they made their England debut — it's ten points for each right answer!

1 DAVID BECKHAM

2 JAMES MILNER

3 JOHN TERRY

4 GARETH BARRY

5 DARREN BENT

2009

2006

2000

1996

2003

MY SCORE... **OUT OF 50**
 MY MATE'S... MY DAD'S...

119

CESC FABREGAS!

Ten points for each right answer on the superstar!

1 What position does he play in?
- **A** Keeper
- **B** Midfielder
- **C** Striker

2 How old will Cesc be when the World Cup starts?
- **A** 23 **B** 26 **C** 29

3 Which one of these is he?
- **A** Arsenal captain
- **B** Spain captain
- **C** Part-time chef

4 What shirt number does he wear for Arsenal?
- **A** 4 **B** 10 **C** 23

5 How many games has Cesc played for Spain?
- **A** 25-35
- **B** 45-55
- **C** 65-75

6 Which footy boots does he wear?
- **A** Adidas
- **B** Nike
- **C** Puma

7 How many World Cups has he played in?
- **A** 0 **B** 1 **C** 2

8 Arsenal signed Cesc when he was 16 – but from which club?
- **A** Tottenham
- **B** Hamburg
- **C** Barcelona

9 What is Cesc's full first name?
- **A** Cescy-Wescy
- **B** Francesc
- **C** Bobcesc

10 Which of these club records does he hold at Arsenal?
- **A** Youngest to play for first team
- **B** Most goals in a season
- **C** Shortest ever player

MY SCORE... **OUT OF 100**

MY MATE'S... MY DAD'S...

120

PREM LINK!

Match these World Cup stars with their Prem clubs - it's ten points for each correct answer!

1 BENOIT ASSOU-EKOTTO
Country: CAMEROON
Club:
....

2 GAEL CLICHY
Country: FRANCE
Club:
....

3 RYAN BABEL
Country: HOLLAND
Club:
....

4 DICKSON ETUHU
Country: NIGERIA
Club:
....

5 ROQUE SANTA CRUZ
Country: PARAGUAY
Club:
....

6 JOSE BOSINGWA
Country: PORTUGAL
Club:
....

7 BENNI McCARTHY
Country: SOUTH AFRICA
Club:
....

8 TIM HOWARD
Country: USA
Club:
....

9 RIO FERDINAND
Country: ENGLAND
Club:
....

10 SEYI OLOFINJANA
Country: NIGERIA
Club:
....

MAN. UNITED
LIVERPOOL
EVERTON
WEST HAM
FULHAM
HULL
MAN. CITY
CHELSEA
TOTTENHAM
ARSENAL

 MY SCORE... **OUT OF 100**

 MY MATE'S... MY DAD'S...

TEAM FOOD CHALLENGE!

Four top World Cup countries need their pre-match meal, but which of these routes will take them to the correct grub? It's 25 points for each right answer!

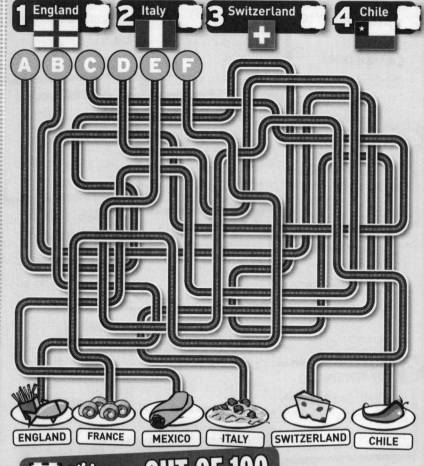

1 England 2 Italy 3 Switzerland 4 Chile

A B C D E F

ENGLAND | FRANCE | MEXICO | ITALY | SWITZERLAND | CHILE

MY SCORE... OUT OF 100

MY MATE'S... **MY DAD'S...**

Circle the odd one out in each of the boxes below – it's 20 points for each correct answer!

1
THREE LIONS   (SWITZERLAND)
THE SAMBA KINGS   THE ELEPHANTS

2
(PETER CROUCH)   TIM HOWARD
TIM CAHILL   STEVEN PIENAAR

3
WAYNE BRIDGE   ROB GREEN
JAMES MILNER   (HUGO RODALLEGA)

4
ADIDAS   NIKE
(LEVI'S)   UMBRO

5
MERCURIAL SUPERFLY II   MIGHTY TWIG
POWERCAT 1.10   (SPECIALI)

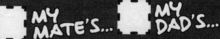

MY SCORE... **OUT OF 100**
MY MATE'S...   MY DAD'S...

123

WHOSE INBOX?

Guess which star is receiving these emails – 50 points if you get it right!

1

Subject: Africa Cup of Nations
From: Sal
Sent: May 2010

Hello big man!

Good luck at the World Cup next month. I hope it makes up for our country's surprise exit in the quarter-finals of the Africa Cup of Nations!

See you in London when you get back,
Sal

2

Subject: Your charity
From: Aruna
Sent: May 2010

Ello No.11!

Really good of you to build that hospital with the money raised from your own charity!

See you soon,
A

3

Subject: Chelsea
From: Joe
Sent: June 2010

Hey dude.

Let me know when you're back in Chelsea after the World Cup so we can meet up!

Laters,
Joe

4

Subject: Longish hair
From: Your hairdressers
Sent: May 2010

Dear Sir,

Will you keep your ponytail for the World Cup, or will you be requiring a haircut? 10% discount this week!

Kind regards,
Enzo

WHO IS IT?

MY SCORE... **OUT OF 50**

MY MATE'S...   MY DAD'S...

CROSSWORD FUN!

It's ten points for each right answer!

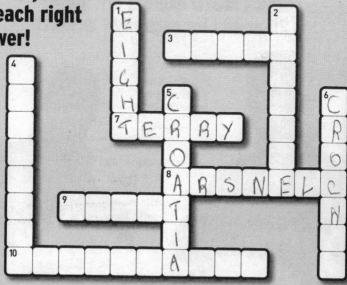

DOWN

1 Frank Lampard's shirt number at Chelsea (5)

2 England and Liverpool right-back, Glen _____ (7)

4 The only other European country drawn in England's World Cup group (8)

5 Country that England thumped 5-1 to qualify for the World Cup (7)

6 Peter _____, ex-England keeper who holds a record 125 England caps (7)

ACROSS

3 England manager _____ Capello (5)

7 John _____ was England captain before Rio Ferdinand (5)

8 Theo Walcott plays for this club (7)

9 African champions that England played in a friendly in March (5)

10 Aston Villa's English striker Gabriel _____ (10)

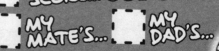

MY SCORE... **OUT OF 100**

MY MATE'S...   MY DAD'S...

125

SAMUEL ETO'O!

Ten points for each right answer on the superstar!

1 Which boots does Samuel Eto'o wear?

A Nike
B Puma
C Umbro

2 He's the all-time top scorer in the history of which tournament?

A Africa Cup of Nations
B Copa America
C Olympics

3 How old is he?
A 29 B 33 C 37

4 Samuel's scored in two different...

A Champions League finals
B World Cup finals
C FA Cup finals

5 What shirt number does he wear for Inter Milan?
A 5 B 7 C 9

6 Barcelona swapped Eto'o, plus cash, for which player?

A Rodallega
B Kaka
C Ibrahimovic

7 What's his nickname?

A Bobby
B Johnny
C Sammy

8 Who is his strike partner at Inter Milan?

A Diego Milito
B Wayne Rooney
C Lionel Messi

9 Which of these clubs has Eto'o NOT played for?

A Inter Milan
B Real Mallorca
C Lyon

10 Samuel scored over 100 league goals for which massive club?

A Man. United
B Barcelona
C Valencia

MY SCORE... OUT OF 100

MY MATE'S... MY DAD'S...

127

TRUE OR FALSE?

1 Scotland won the World Cup back in 1974!

True False

2 As hosts, South Africa automatically qualified for this year's World Cup!

True False

3 Liverpool midfielder Yossi Benayoun plays for Honduras!

True False

4 Brazil have won the World Cup more than any other country!

True False

5 Switzerland's nickname is the Cheeses With Holes In!

True False

MY SCORE...

QUALIFIED?

Put a tick next to the country if they made it to South Africa or a cross if they didn't – it's ten points for each!

1 CZECH REPUBLIC

Did they qualify?

2 GHANA

Did they qualify?

3 SOUTH AFRICA

Did they qualify?

4 BULGARIA

Did they qualify?

Which facts are true and which are false? It's ten points for each correct answer!

6 Chelsea defender Branislav Ivanovic plays for Serbia!

True False

7 Andrey Arshavin won't be playing in the World Cup!

True False

8 France's home shirt is red!

True False

9 Spain have never won the World Cup!

True False

10 Turkey came third in the 2002 World Cup!

True False

OUT OF 100 ☐ **MY MATE'S...** ☐ **MY DAD'S...**

5 POLAND
Did they qualify? ☐

6 AUSTRALIA
Did they qualify? ☐

7 HOLLAND
Did they qualify? ☐

9 SLOVAKIA
Did they qualify? ☐

10 COLOMBIA
Did they qualify? ☐

8 BELGIUM
Did they qualify? ☐

MY SCORE... OUT OF 100

MY MATE'S... **MY DAD'S...**

10 QUESTIONS ON ITALY

Ten points for each correct answer!

1 What colour is Italy's home shirt?
- **A** Blue
- **B** Red
- **C** White

2 Who's their No.1 goalkeeper?
- **A** Gianluigi Buffon
- **B** Igor Akinfeev
- **C** Iker Casillas

3 Midfielder Andrea Pirlo plays for which club?
- **A** AC Milan
- **B** Bayern Munich
- **C** Hamburg

4 When was the last time Italy won the World Cup?
- **A** 1998
- **B** 2002
- **C** 2006

5 Which of these Premier League clubs does Alberto Aquilani play for?
- **A** Chelsea
- **B** Liverpool
- **C** Everton

6 Who captains the Italy team?
- **A** Alberto Gilardino
- **B** Antonio Di Natale
- **C** Fabio Cannavaro

7 What is Italy's nickname?
- **A** Wazzaria
- **B** Azzurri
- **C** Gazza-Bazza

8 How many times have Italy won the World Cup?
- **A** 2 **B** 4 **C** 6

9 What colour is Italy's away shirt?
- **A** White
- **B** Blue
- **C** Gold

10 Which position does Giuseppe Rossi play in?
- **A** Defence
- **B** Midfield
- **C** Attack

MY SCORE... **OUT OF 100**

MY MATE'S...

MY DAD'S...

130

WORLD CUP WINNERS!

Tick next to the stars who have won the World Cup or cross those who haven't — it's ten points for each!

1 RONALDINHO
Brazil
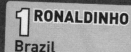

2 STEVEN GERRARD
England

3 THIERRY HENRY
France

4 FRANCESCO TOTTI
Italy

5 ROBIN VAN PERSIE
Holland

6 ROMAN PAVLYUCHENKO
Russia

7 LUCIO
Brazil

8 FERNANDO TORRES
Spain

9 FABIO CANNAVARO
Italy

10 ABOU DIABY
France

MY SCORE... OUT OF 100

MY MATE'S...   MY DAD'S...

WHO AM I?

Can you guess the star from these clues? It's 50 points if you're right!

My shirt number for the Reds is No.18!

I scored the only goal in the Merseyside derby in February!

I'm usually a winger for Liverpool, but I can also play up front!

I always wear black footy boots!

I'm a hard-working player!

I have curly blond hair!

I've played over 50 times for Holland!

I'm 29 years old!

WHO IS IT?

....

MY SCORE... OUT OF 50

MY MATE'S...

MY DAD'S...

JOHN TERRY!

1 Which of these is John Terry?

A Chelsea's top scorer
B Chelsea's oldest player
C Chelsea's captain

2 When Terry scored against Ukraine, what did Wayne Rooney pretend to do to him?

A Cut JT's hair
B Polish JT's boots
C Tell him off

3 What shirt number does JT have on his back at Chelsea?

A 4   B 26   C 13

5 Which of these finals has he played in?

A Champions League
B World Cup
C Euro 2008

4 In which year did Terry make his England debut?

A 1998
B 2003
C 2008

MY SCORE...

LINK-UP PLAY

**Put a block from Group A
One's already been done**

GROUP A

FABR	AQUI	
FOOT	PORT	~~PALA~~
CAME	SLOV	PARA
MIDF	CROS	CASI

| A | B |
| PALA | CIOS |

EGAS

GROUP B

| ~~CIOS~~ | LLAS | GUAY | SBAR | LANI |
| IELD | BALL | AKIA | UGAL | ROON |

134

It's ten points each for each right answer on the England star!

6 What is John Terry's position?

A Right-back
B Centre-back
C Left-back

7 Which of these did JT used to be?

A Arsenal captain
B England captain
C England coach

8 Which boots does he wear?

A Nike
B Adidas
C Umbro

9 With which club did he make his debut?

A Tottenham
B Fulham
C Chelsea

10 In 2007 he became the first captain to lift the FA Cup...

A At the new Wembley
B With his kid in it
C With his left hand

OUT OF 100 ☐ MY MATE'S... ☐ MY DAD'S...

next to a block from Group B to make a World Cup word. for you – it's ten points for each pair you get right!

Ⓐ Ⓑ Ⓐ Ⓑ Ⓐ Ⓑ Ⓐ Ⓑ

☐ MY SCORE... **OUT OF 100**
☐ MY MATE'S... ☐ MY DAD'S...

135

TEAM SHEET!

Fill in the gaps and get ten points for each one!

2010 WORLD CUP GROUP B
ARGENTINA V NIGERIA
SATURDAY 12 JUNE

ARGENTINA

Sergio ROMERO	GK	AZ Alkmaar
Javier ZANETTI	DF	..... Milan
Martin DEMICHELIS	DF	...... Munich
Nicolas OTAMENDI	DF	V. Sarsfield
Gabriel HEINZE	DF	Marseille
Javier .... (C)	MF	Liverpool
Juan Seb. VERON	MF	Estudiantes
Angel DI MARIA	MF	Benfica
Maxi RODRIGUEZ	MF	....
...... MESSI	ST	....
Carlos TEVEZ	ST	... .

SUBSTITUTES

Mariano ANDUJAR,
Emiliano INSUA, Jonas GUTIERREZ,
Gonzalo HIGUAIN, Sergio AGUERO

MANAGER

Diego MARADONA

NIGERIA

Vincent ENYEAMA	GK	Hapoel Tel Aviv
Chidi ODIAH	DF	CSKA Moscow
Taye TAIWO	DF	Marseille
Joseph YOBO	DF	....
Danny SHITTU	DF	Bolton
Seyi OLOFINJANA	MF	Hull
John Obi	MF	Chelsea
Dickson ETUHU	MF	Fulham
Peter ODEMWINGIE	ST	Lokomotiv Moscow
Obafemi MARTINS	ST	Wolfsburg
YAKUBU (C)	ST	....

SUBSTITUTES

Austin EJIDE, Obinna NWANERI,
Ayila YUSSUF, Victor ANICHEBE,
Nwankwo KANU

MANAGER

Lars LAGERBÄCK

MY MATE'S... MY DAD'S...

MY SCORE... OUT OF 100

136

MYSTERY MOBILE!

Which top superstar owns this mobile phone? 50 points if you get it right!

GOOD LUCK WITH ENGLAND IN UR 1ST WORLD CUP!

10 YRS SINCE UR ENGLAND DEBUT! UR GETTING OLD, MATE!

GAZ BAZ, U LEFT MANCHESTER 4 SOUTH AFRICA YET?

AS A DEF MID, WATCH OUT 4 ATTACKING PLAYERS AT THE WC!

YO CITY'S NO.18! FANCY PLAYING ON THE WII?

WHO IS IT?

. . . .

MY SCORE...

OUT OF 50

MY MATE'S...

MY DAD'S...

MEGA WORDSEARCH!

Can you find the 20 international managers that are hiding below? Five points for each name you can find

Antic

Bradley

Capello

Del Bosque

Domenech

Dunga

Hitzfeld

Huh

Kek

Le Guen

Lippi

Low

Maradona

Martino

Okada

Olsen

Queiroz

Saadane

Tabarez

Verbeek

B	J	L	I	P	P	I	D	F	A	O	V	B	B	E
R	C	E	S	E	U	Q	S	O	B	L	E	D	L	Q
A	W	S	J	I	B	A	N	G	T	R	D	R	F	U
D	D	K	A	W	D	R	B	O	D	U	N	G	A	E
L	O	P	G	A	D	B	F	L	E	G	U	E	N	I
E	M	N	K	D	D	L	X	E	R	B	B	B	T	R
Y	E	O	K	L	M	A	R	A	D	O	N	A	V	O
X	N	C	M	E	M	Y	N	Q	Y	E	U	D	S	Z
M	E	Z	G	F	G	B	L	E	C	Z	N	I	T	C
U	C	C	I	Z	D	O	H	L	I	H	U	H	A	I
U	H	S	U	T	W	Y	G	Y	F	C	K	G	K	T
F	V	C	R	I	D	K	E	E	B	R	E	V	Q	N
R	T	Y	R	H	P	C	D	T	M	R	K	B	J	A
N	E	S	L	O	Z	H	Z	E	R	A	B	A	T	F
J	C	A	P	E	L	L	O	O	N	I	T	R	A	M

MY SCORE... OUT OF 100

MY MATE'S...   MY DAD'S...

138

GUESS THE AGE!

Match the England player to their age and grab ten points for each correct answer!

1 WAYNE ROONEY
How old is he?

2 ROBERT GREEN
How old is he?

3 JERMAIN DEFOE
How old is he?

4 DAVID JAMES
How old is he?

5 AARON LENNON
How old is he?

A 30

B 27

C 23

D 24

E 39

MY SCORE... **OUT OF 50**

MY MATE'S...

MY DAD'S...

JOIN THE DOTS!

Link these dots together to uncover a star in action!

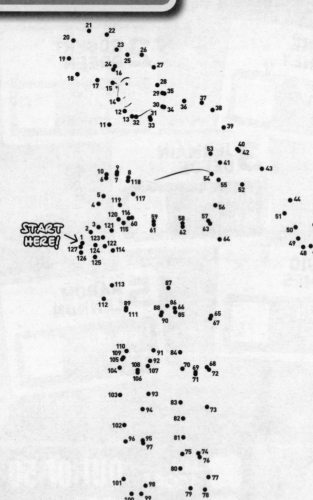

START HERE!

WHO AM I?

Can you name this star from these clues? Get 50 points if you're right!

My full first name is Clinton!

I usually play on the right-wing, but can also play up front!

My hip-hop name is Deuce!

I missed a lot of the season through injury!

I wear Nike soccer boots!

I play for Fulham!

Hey guys! I'm from the USA!

I'm 27 years old!

WHO IS IT?

....

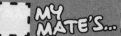

MY SCORE... **OUT OF 50**

MY MATE'S...

MY DAD'S...

ROBINHO!

Ten points for each right answer on the superstar!

1 The Man. City superstar spent half of the season on loan to which club?

A Santos
B Bayern Munich
C River Plate

2 How much did Man. City pay for him in 2008?

A £5.5m
B £25.5m
C £32.5m

3 Which of these celebrations is Robinho most famous for?

A Doing a cartwheel
B Sucking his thumb
C Somersaulting

4 How many games has Robinho played for Brazil?

A 30-40
B 50-60
C 70-80

5 Robinho is actually his nickname. What's his full name?

A Robson de Souza
B Ribena de Juice
C Robert a la Carte

6 Which footy boots does he wear?

A Puma
B Nike
C Adidas

7 How old is Robinho?

A 22 B 26 C 30

8 What did he win in 2009 with Brazil?

A World Cup
B Copa America
C Confederations Cup

9 City signed him from which club?

A Atletico Madrid
B Barcelona
C Real Madrid

10 Which of the following leagues has he won?

A La Liga
B Premier League
C Serie A

 MY SCORE... **OUT OF 100**

 MY MATE'S... MY DAD'S...

JUMBLED UP!

Work out the names of these England stars – grab ten points for each correct answer!

1. ANDINFERD
2. CHOURC
3. RETRY
4. ELOC
5. BRARY
6. LAMDRAP
7. NEYROO
8. GREDARR
9. DOFEE
10. LONENN

MY SCORE... **OUT OF 100**

MY MATE'S...   MY DAD'S...

143

NAME GAME!

Do you know these five players? Fill in the missing letters on their shirts – 20 points for each!

ARR

4 ①

ENGLAND

_NEL_A

② **9**

FRANCE

_ILLA

③ **7**

SPAIN

DON_VA_

10

④

USA

SK_TE_

11 ⑤

SLOVAKIA

MY SCORE... **OUT OF 100**

MY MATE'S... MY DAD'S...

DADS V LADS

Get your dad to answer the questions on the left while you do the right – ten points for each correct answer!

1994

1 Which Brazilian was voted the best player of the 1994 World Cup?

2 Which country hosted the tournament?

3 Which Scandinavian country came third in the tournament?

4 Who scored the Republic of Ireland's winning goal against Italy?

5 How far did England get in the '94 World Cup?

NOW

1 Which Brazilian goal machine has been tearing it up in Spain for Sevilla?

2 Which USA star also plays for Fulham?

3 Which one of these three teams will be at the World Cup – Denmark, Finland or Norway?

4 The Italy boss is called Marcello L_____!

5 Which England player is nicknamed JT?

MY SCORE... OUT OF 50 MY DAD'S...

145

TRUE OR FALSE?

Which facts are true and which are false? Circle the right answers – it's ten points for each one!

1 The only year Wales qualified for a World Cup was in 1958!

True False

2 Liverpool forward Dirk Kuyt plays for Holland!

True False

3 The USA's nickname is the Barack Obamas!

True False

4 There will be 32 countries at this summer's World Cup!

True False

5 The Wolves striker Kevin Doyle plays for New Zealand!

True False

6 Presenter Jake Humphrey played for Northern Ireland in the 1994 World Cup!

True False

7 South Africa v Mexico will be the first game of this year's World Cup!

True False

8 Sunderland striker Darren Bent plays for Portugal!

True False

9 Portugal have never won the World Cup!

True False

10 Germany's home shirt is blue!

True False

MY SCORE... **OUT OF 100**

 MY MATE'S... MY DAD'S...

WHOSE INBOX?

Guess which star is receiving these emails – 50 points if you get it right!

1

Subject: Bonjour!
From: Thierry
Sent: April 2010

Bonjour monsieur!

Good luck at the World Cup – you may need it because at the age of 31, you're no spring chicken!

T

2

Subject: In London!
From: Forgetful Franck
Sent: April 2010

Wassup dude!

Just checking – you're at Chelsea now, right? You've been at so many different clubs, it's hard to remember!

Best wishes,
Franck

3

Subject: Goal machine!
From: Yoann
Sent: May 2010

Good luck at ze World Cup!

After winning ze Prem Golden Boot in 2009, maybe you can also win ze World Cup's Golden Boot!

Au revoir,
Yoann

4

Subject: Your famous celebration
From: Claude
Sent: May 2010

Just a quick message, mate.

Carry on celebrating goals by turning your hands into the shape of a dove – I love that one!

Cheers,
Claude-meister

WHO IS IT?

@

....

MY SCORE... OUT OF 50

MY MATE'S...   MY DAD'S...

147

MATCH OF THE DAY MAGAZINE WORLD CUP QUIZ BOOK!

TEAM BUS CHALLENGE!

Four top World Cup stars are late for a game, but which route will lead them to the correct team bus? It's 25 points for each one you get right!

1 Nani **2** Frank Lampard **3** Dirk Kuyt **4** William Gallas

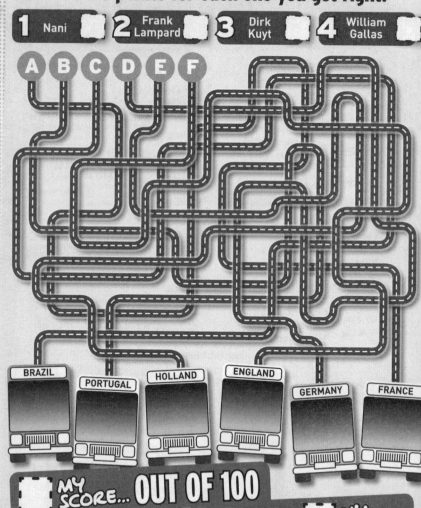

A B C D E F

BRAZIL PORTUGAL HOLLAND ENGLAND GERMANY FRANCE

MY SCORE... **OUT OF 100**

MY MATE'S... MY DAD'S...

148

ODD ONE OUT!

Circle the odd one out in each of the boxes below – it's 20 points for each right answer!

1
FABIO CAPELLO DAVID BECKHAM
DIEGO MARADONA MARCELLO LIPPI

2
RIO FERDINAND MICHAEL BALLACK
IKER CASILLAS DAVID VILLA

3
ROBERT HUTH DECO
DIDIER DROGBA MICHAEL ESSIEN

4
JOHANNESBURG DURBAN
CAPE TOWN WEMBLEY

5
WAYNE ROONEY JERMAIN DEFOE
PETER CROUCH MATTHEW UPSON

MY SCORE... OUT OF 100

MY MATE'S... **MY DAD'S...**

149

FRANCK RIBERY!

Ten points for each right answer on the superstar!

1 Which of these features does Franck have?

A Short brown hair
B A massive mole on his nose
C A massive earring

2 What position does he play in?

A Goal
B Defence
C Wing

3 What shirt number does he wear for his club Bayern Munich?

A 7 B 8 C 9

4 When did Franck win his first international cap?

A 2002
B 2006
C 2010

5 Which of these clubs have NOT been linked with a move for him?

A Chelsea
B Real Madrid
C Burnley

6 How many matches has he played for France?

A 10-20
B 40-50
C 70-80

7 Which footy boots does Franck wear?

A Nike
B Umbro
C Adidas

8 How many World Cups has he played in before this year?

A 0 B 1 C 2

9 Which of these clubs has Franck never played for?

A Marseille
B Galatasaray
C Liverpool

10 How old is he?

A 19 B 23 C 27

MY SCORE... **OUT OF 100**

MY MATE'S... MY DAD'S...

150

WHOSE INBOX?

Guess which star is receiving these emails – 50 points if you get it right!

1

Subject: Merseyside BBQ
From: Manuel
Sent: May 2010

Hola!

Why don't you and your neighbour, Fernando Torres, come round mine for a barbeque tonight? It'll be a good luck meal before the World Cup!

Manuel

2

Subject: No.25
From: Fernando
Sent: May 2010

Hey baldy!

I got your number, 25, printed on the back of my keeper's shirt today. Good luck in South Africa!

F

3

Subject: Spain
From: Daniel
Sent: May 2010

Hey up big man!

Good luck at the World Cup! I'm sure you'll play a massive role for Spain, but it will be hard beating Iker Casillas to get into the starting line-up!

All the best, Daniel

4

Subject: Liverpool
From: Jamie
Sent: May 2010

Alreet, lad!

Let me know when you're back in Liverpool. I'm moving house so I could do with a safe pair of hands to help!

Cheers, la!
J-Man

WHO IS IT?

....

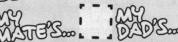

MY SCORE... OUT OF 50

MY MATE'S...   MY DAD'S...

151

TRUE OR FALSE?

Which facts are true and which are false? Circle the right answers – it's ten points for each one!

1 Northern Ireland have qualified for three World Cups in their history!

True False

2 Uruguay's home shirt is pink!

True False

3 Man. City star Craig Bellamy plays for New Zealand!

True False

4 Brazil are the only country to have played in every single World Cup!

True False

5 Chelsea midfielder Deco plays for Portugal!

True False

6 France have never won the World Cup!

True False

7 Ryan Giggs has never played in a World Cup!

True False

8 Lionel Messi plays for Argentina!

True False

9 Germany have reached the semi-finals more than any other country!

True False

10 Greece have never scored a goal in the World Cup!

True False

MY SCORE... **OUT OF 100**

MY MATE'S...

MY DAD'S...

152

QUALIFIED?

Tick the countries that made it to South Africa and cross those that didn't – grab ten points for each!

1 USA
Did they qualify?

2 FINLAND
Did they qualify?

3 INDIA
Did they qualify?

4 CAMEROON
Did they qualify?

5 NORWAY
Did they qualify?

6 UKRAINE
Did they qualify?

7 EGYPT
Did they qualify?

8 HONDURAS
Did they qualify?

9 URUGUAY
Did they qualify?

10 SWITZERLAND
Did they qualify?

MY SCORE... **OUT OF 100**

MY MATE'S...

MY DAD'S...

10 QUESTIONS ON

Ten points for each correct answer!

1 What colour is Germany's home shirt?

- **A** White
- **B** Black
- **C** Red

2 True or false – Germany were undefeated in qualifying!

- **A** True
- **B** False

3 Which one of these players is the Germany captain?

- **A** Thomas Hitzlsperger
- **B** Michael Ballack
- **C** Lukas Podolski

4 Who's the Germany boss?

- **A** Joachim High
- **B** Joachim Middle
- **C** Joachim Low

5 When did they last reach a World Cup final?

A 1998 **B** 2002 **C** 2006

MY SCORE...

RAPPING ROWS!

1 Argentina striker plays for Man. _____

2 Holland and Arsenal striker Robin van _____

3 Spain and Barcelona midfielder whose name starts with X _____

4 Australia and Fulham keeper _____ Schwarzer

5 England star James Milner plays home club games at Villa _____

6 Floodlights are turned on when it's _____

1	2	3
4	5	6
7	8	9
10	11	12

GERMANY!

6 German defender Robert Huth is at which Prem club?

A Chelsea
B Fulham
C Stoke

7 Who beat Germany in the Euro 2008 final?

A Spain
B Italy
C France

8 Which current Germany player has scored ten goals in two World Cups?

A Cacau
B Miroslav Klose
C Patrick Helmes

9 Germany is the only country in history to have won...

A The men's and women's World Cups
B Eight World Cups
C Ten Euro championships

10 Midfielder Bastian Schweinsteiger plays for which club?

A Bayern Munich
B Barcelona
C Man. United

OUT OF 100 ☐ MY MATE'S... ☐ MY DAD'S...

Write the answers to the clues in the spaces below – they all rhyme. Grab 25 points for each group!

7 Italy captain Fabio _____
8 West Ham's Guillermo Franco plays for this country _____
9 Surname of a Tottenham and England striker _____

10 Country that won the 2006 World Cup _____
11 Switzerland and West Ham's Valon _____
12 South American country that sounds really cold _____

☐ MY SCORE... OUT OF 100
☐ MY MATE'S... ☐ MY DAD'S...

COUNTRY CONNECT!

Try and match the World Cup stars to the countries they play for – it's ten points for each pair you join up correctly!

1 KAKA

2 FRANCK RIBERY

3 XAVI

4 MIROSLAV KLOSE

5 LIONEL MESSI

6 ANDREA PIRLO

7 WESLEY SNEIJDER

8 DIEGO FORLAN

9 CRISTIANO RONALDO

10 STEVEN GERRARD

A FRANCE   **B** GERMANY   **C** ARGENTINA

D URUGUAY   **E** HOLLAND

F BRAZIL   **G** ENGLAND   **H** ITALY

I PORTUGAL

J SPAIN

MY SCORE... **OUT OF 100**

MY MATE'S...   MY DAD'S...

157

GARETH BARRY!

Ten points for each right answer on the superstar!

1 How much did Man. City pay to buy Gareth Barry in 2009?

A £5m
B £12m
C £19m

2 What position does he play in?

A Central midfield
B Centre-back
C Right-back

3 Barry was at which club for 12 years before joining Man. City?

A Newcastle
B Man. United
C Aston Villa

4 Which of these teams did he NOT score against in 2009-10?

A Stoke
B Man. United
C Bolton

5 What shirt number does he wear at City?

A 18 B 14 C 25

6 When did he make his England debut?

A 1996
B 2000
C 2006

7 In 2007, Barry became the youngest player in history to...

A Play 300 Prem games
B Score for England
C Captain Man. City

8 Which club tried to beat Man. City to the signing of Barry?

A Man. United
B Chelsea
C Liverpool

9 Which of these has Gareth won?

A Carling Cup
B Premier League
C Neither

10 How old is he?

A 14 B 29 C 34

MY SCORE... **OUT OF 100**
MY MATE'S...
MY DAD'S...

MYSTERY MOBILE!

Which World Cup star owns this mobile phone? 50 points if you get it right!

GOOD LUCK 4 ENGLAND AT UR 2ND EVER WORLD CUP!

WOT U DOING 4 UR 32ND BIRTHDAY DURING THE WORLD CUP?

C U BACK AT CHELSEA NEXT SEASON, MATE!

4 TOP GOALS IN QUALIFYING - HOPE U SCORE LOADS IN SA!

JUST READ UR BOOK, TOTALLY FRANK. IT'S A GREAT READ!

WHO IS IT?
....

MY SCORE...
OUT OF 50
MY MATE'S...
MY DAD'S...

159

MEGA WORDSEARCH!

Can you find 20 clubs that some of the World Cup play for stars? It's five points for each team you find!

AC Milan

Arsenal

Aston Villa

Barcelona

Bayern Munich

Boca Juniors

Chelsea

Everton

Fiorentina

Inter Milan

A	R	S	E	N	A	L	A	B	G	X	Z	W	E	B
Q	A	Z	C	L	O	O	P	R	E	V	I	L	X	A
B	O	C	A	J	U	N	I	O	R	S	S	D	F	Y
B	N	O	O	M	A	I	C	N	E	L	A	V	X	E
R	E	A	L	M	A	D	R	I	D	D	Y	X	P	R
X	R	T	J	M	A	N	U	N	I	T	E	D	V	N
B	V	G	T	Y	K	L	C	H	E	L	S	E	A	M
A	L	P	P	O	R	T	O	I	X	U	I	O	P	U
R	Y	S	R	E	F	E	J	V	T	X	M	N	E	N
C	O	V	A	H	G	V	D	X	A	Y	S	D	F	I
E	N	I	I	N	T	E	R	M	I	L	A	N	N	C
L	X	X	F	I	O	R	E	N	T	I	N	A	X	H
O	R	F	C	A	S	T	O	N	V	I	L	L	A	B
N	Z	Z	O	O	T	O	T	T	E	N	H	A	M	R
A	C	M	I	L	A	N	G	S	E	V	I	L	L	A

Liverpool

Lyon

Man. City

Man. United

Porto

PSV

Real Madrid

Sevilla

Tottenham

Valencia

MY SCORE... OUT OF 100

MY MATE'S...

MY DAD'S...

160

COOL FINISHING!

Fit a set of three letters into the correct footy word below – it's ten points for each right answer!

MAN

APT

STA

MID

FIN

VOL

URY

ACK

TIC

EPE

1				D	I	U	M
2				A	L		
3	I	N	J				
4	C			A	I	N	
5				A	G	E	R
6	T	A	C				S
7	K	E			R		
8	T			L	E		
9				L	E	Y	
10			F	I	E	L	D

MY SCORE... **OUT OF 100**

MY MATE'S...

MY DAD'S...

SHADY PIC!

Shade in each area that contains two dots to reveal a footy picture!

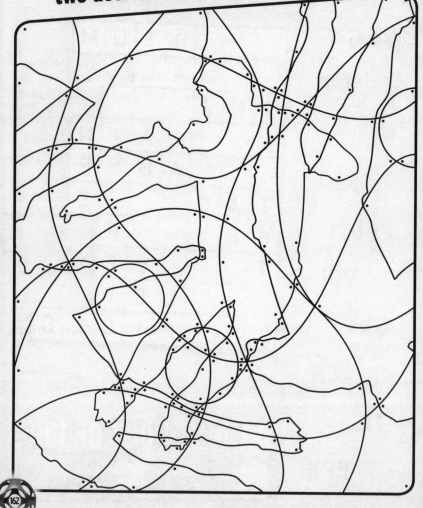

162

TEAM SHEET!

Fill in the gaps and get ten points for each one!

2010 WORLD CUP GROUP H
SPAIN v SWITZERLAND
WEDNESDAY 16 JUNE

SPAIN

Iker .... (C)	GK	Real Madrid
Joan CAPDEVILA	DF	Villarreal
Carles PUYOL	DF	Barcelona
Gerard PIQUE	DF	Barcelona
Sergio RAMOS	DF	....
XAVI	MF	....
Xabi ALONSO	MF	.... Madrid
...... INIESTA	MF	Barcelona
David SILVA	MF	Valencia
.... TORRES	ST	....
David VILLA	ST	....

SWITZERLAND

Diego BENAGLIO	GK	Wolfsburg
Steph LICHTSTEINER	DF	Lazio
Philippe SENDEROS	DF	Arsenal
Stephane GRICHTING	DF	Auxerre
Christoph SPYCHER	DF	Frankfurt
Gelson FERNANDES	MF	Saint-Etienne
Gokhan INLER	MF	Udinese
Valon BEHRAMI	MF	....
Tranquillo BARNETTA	MF	Bayer L'kusen
Alexander FREI (C)	ST	Basel
Eren DERDIYOK	ST	Bayer L'kusen

SUBSTITUTES

Pepe REINA, Carlos MARCHENA,
Marcos SENNA, ... FABREGAS,
Dani GUIZA

SUBSTITUTES

Marco WOLFLI, Johan DJOUROU,
Marco PADALINO, Johan VONLANTHEN,
Blaise NKUFO

MANAGER Vicente DEL BOSQUE   **MANAGER** Ottmar HITZFELD

MY SCORE... OUT OF 100

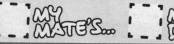

MY MATE'S...   MY DAD'S

163

WHO AM I?

Can you name the star from these clues? It's 50 points if you're right!

WHO IS IT?

....

MY SCORE... OUT OF 50

MY MATE'S...

MY DAD'S...

SHOOTING PRACTICE!

Write your answers in the target to reveal a name around the outer letters – get 50 points if you find it!

TIP! Answers start from the outer edge and go towards the centre so that each one ends with the letter S!

1 Germany and France committed the most _____ at the 2006 World Cup (5)

2 Barcelona and Spain midfielder, _____ Iniesta (6)

3 England and Everton left-back, Leighton _____ (6)

4 Real Madrid and Spain's long-haired right-back, Sergio _____ (5)

5 Robin van Persie plays his home club games here (8)

6 Arsenal and France centre-back, William _____ (6)

7 Brazil and Barcelona right-back, Dani _____ (5)

8 The nickname of Jermain Defoe's club (5)

PLAYER'S NAME:

....

MY SCORE... **OUT OF 50**

MY MATE'S...

MY DAD'S...

JAVIER MASCHERANO!

Ten points for each right answer on the superstar!

1 How much did Liverpool pay to buy the Argentina star in 2008?

A £2.7m
B £12.5m
C £18.6m

2 Which one of these is Mascherano's nickname?

A Masch
B Javs
C Argy-bargy

3 Which one of these positions does he play in?

A Central midfield
B Centre-back
C Left-back

4 Which of these is Mascherano?

A Liverpool's youngest player
B Argentina captain
C Argentina player/coach

5 Which of these Prem clubs did he play for in the 2006-07 season?

A Everton
B Sunderland
C West Ham

6 What shirt number does he wear for Liverpool?

A 20   B 25   C 30

7 Which of these clubs has he played for in the past?

A Sporting Lisbon
B River Plate
C Benfica

8 Which of these has he won?

A Olympic gold
B World Cup
C Euro 2008

9 Against which club was he NOT shown a red card this season?

A Portsmouth
B Man. United
C Tottenham

10 In which year did he make his debut for Argentina?

A 1991
B 1997
C 2003

MY SCORE... **OUT OF 100**

MY MATE'S...   MY DAD'S...

CROSSWORD FUN!

It's ten points for each right answer!

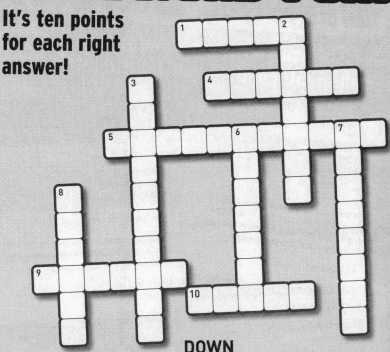

ACROSS

1 Nigeria's home shirt colour (5)

4 Ivory Coast striker Didier _____ (6)

5 Country that's hosting the 2010 World Cup (5, 6)

9 The Prem club of Ghana defender John Paintsil (6)

10 Michael Essien plays for this country (5)

DOWN

2 African nation nicknamed the Super Eagles (7)

3 This country's nickname is The Elephants (5, 5)

6 The African country in England's World Cup group (7)

7 Arsenal's Alexandre Song plays for this country (8)

8 Cameroon striker _____ Eto'o (6)

MY SCORE... **OUT OF 100**

MY MATE'S...

MY DAD'S...

167

WHOSE INBOX?

Guess which star is receiving these emails – 50 points if you get it right!

1

Subject: Ankle problems
From: Edgar van Dutch
Sent: May 2010

Hi!

How's your ankle now? You missed a lot of the season with that injury. Hopefully you'll be banging the goals in for Holland again, though!

All the best, Edgar

2

Subject: No.11
From: Ronald
Sent: May 2010

Greetings from Holland,

I hear you shall be the lone striker for the Oranje. Will your shirt number be 11 like at your club in north London?

Thank you lots,
Ronald

3

Subject: Adidas footy boots
From: Edwin
Sent: May 2010

Ahoy!

You forgot your Adidas footy boots, so I posted them over to the Holland training camp straight away!

Peace,
Ed

4

Subject: Deadly free-kicks
From: Frank
Sent: May 2010

Rob!

I've got World Cup tickets! I look forward to seeing one of your deadly free-kicks!

See you out there, greasy head!
Frank

WHO IS IT?

MY SCORE... **OUT OF 50**

MY MATE'S...

MY DAD'S...

168

PREM LINK!

Match these stars at the World Cup with their Prem clubs - ten points for each correct answer!

1 DECO
Country: PORTUGAL
Club:
....

2 STEWART DOWNING
Country: ENGLAND
Club:
....

3 MARTIN SKRTEL
Country: SLOVAKIA
Club:
....

4 HENDRY THOMAS
Country: HONDURAS
Club:
....

5 ALEXANDRE SONG
Country: CAMEROON
Club:
....

6 THOMAS SORENSEN
Country: DENMARK
Club:
....

7 TIM HOWARD
Country: USA
Club:
....

8 WES BROWN
Country: ENGLAND
Club:
....

9 VALON BEHRAMI
Country: SWITZERLAND
Club:
....

10 NENAD MILIJAS
Country: SERBIA
Club:
....

WEST HAM

ARSENAL

MAN. UNITED

CHELSEA

ASTON VILLA

STOKE

EVERTON

WOLVES

WIGAN

LIVERPOOL

MY SCORE... **OUT OF 100**

MY MATE'S...

MY DAD'S...

169

LINK-UP PLAY

Put a block from Group A
One's already been done

GROUP A

LAM	RON	
ROB	CAP	~~PIE~~
FAB	DEM	JOH
GER	INI	BAL

GROUP B

~~NAAR~~	LACK	PARD	PSEY	ALDO
RARD	INHO	ESTA	ELLO	NSON

A	B
PIE	NAAR

IANO

COUNTRY CONNECT!

Match the
countries

1 LUIS FABIANO

2 FLORENT MALOUDA

3 ANDRES INIESTA

6 RICARDO CARVALHO

4 DIEGO MILITO

5 RAFAEL VAN DER VAART

9 JOHN TERRY

7 CARLOS VELA

8 PHILIPPE SENDEROS

10 LANDON DONOVAN

next to a block from Group B to make a **World Cup** word.
for you – it's ten points for each pair you get right!

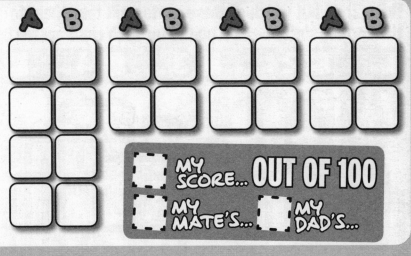

A	B	A	B	A	B	A	B

MY SCORE... **OUT OF 100**

MY MATE'S... MY DAD'S...

World Cup stars with their World Cup
– it's ten points for each correct answer!

A PORTUGAL   **B** SPAIN   **C** BRAZIL

D HOLLAND   **E** USA   **F** SWITZERLAND

G FRANCE   **H** ENGLAND

I MEXICO

J ARGENTINA

MY SCORE... **OUT OF 100**

MY MATE'S... MY DAD'S...

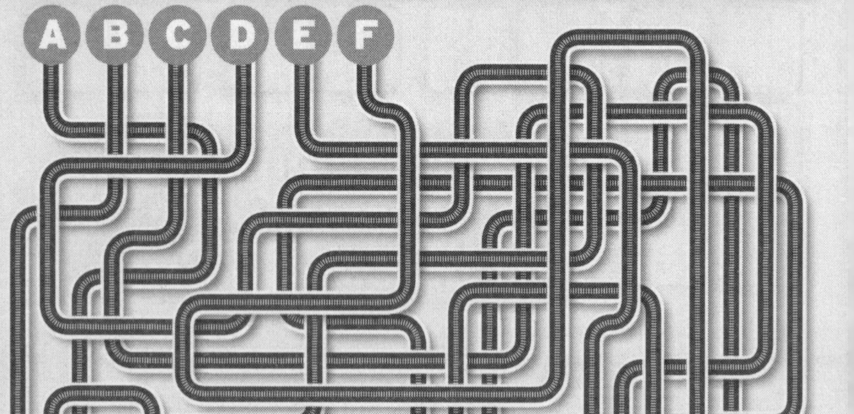

TRANSFER CONNECT!

Match these World Cup stars with the transfer fees they were bought for – it's 25 points for each one you get right!

1 JAMES MILNER
England winger

Newcastle to Aston Villa

£ _ _ _ _ _ _ _

2 ROBINHO
Brazil striker

Real Madrid to Man. City

£ _ _ _ _ _ _ _

3 NEMANJA VIDIC
Serbia defender

Spartak Moscow to Man. United

£ _ _ _ _ _ _ _

4 SOTIRIOS KYRGIAKOS
Greece defender

AEK Athens to Liverpool

£ _ _ _ _ _ _ _

A £7M **B** £2M

C £32.5M **D** £12.5M

MY SCORE... **OUT OF 100**

MY MATE'S... MY DAD'S...

173

GIANLUIGI BUFFON!

1 The Juventus and Italy keeper has which colour hair?

A Black ✓
B Blond
C Ginger

2 How many clean sheets did Gianluigi keep at the 2006 World Cup?

A 1 **B** 5 ✓ **C** 9

3 True or false – he has broken the 100-cap barrier for Italy!

A True ✓
B False

4 What is his shirt number at Serie A Juventus?

A 1 **B** 13 **C** 25

5 Which of these clubs has he played for?

A Lazio
B Sampdoria
C Parma ✓

MY SCORE...

JUMBLED UP!

1 RESTOR

2 GASBREFA

3 ACKBALL

4 ELKANA

5 NAV PERIES

6 HOROBIN

Take ten points each for each right answer on the superstar!

6 How old is the Italy star?
A 27 B 32 ✓ C 37

7 How many games has he played for Juve?
A 150-199 ✓
B 200-249
C 250-300

8 Buffon was named Italy's _____ for Euro 2008!
A Captain ✓
B Manager
C Physio

9 When did he make his Italy debut?
A 1897
B 1997 ✓
C 2007

10 Which of these has he won?
A Champions League ✓
B World Cup
C Euro 2008

OUT OF 100  MY MATE'S...  MY DAD'S...

Can you unscramble these World Cup stars? It's ten points for each right answer!

7 ROLDANO

8 SEMIS

9 VEZET

10 ROGBAD

MY SCORE... **OUT OF 100**
MY MATE'S...
MY DAD'S...

MEGA WORDSEARCH!

Can you find the 20 keepers that are hiding below? It's five points for each name you find!

Adler

Benaglio

Bravo

Buffon

Casillas

Cesar

Eduardo

Enyeama

Handanovic

Howard

Kameni

Lloris

Mucha

Ochoa

Romero

Schwarzer

Sorensen

Stojkovic

Tzorvas

Villar

```
T J T H Y H P B D A H C U M L
H H O S T O J K O V I C B U R
O L A R E Z R A W H C S F K A
W K B N F J S O R E N S E N H
A P B A D L E R O R O M E R O
R E A U O A R C D G C E S L Q
D B D B B G N E N Y E A M A I
L E R U F L I O J Y V S K I B
X N V G A A Y N V R F A W U R
I A I C U R F O O I S L L Y A
N G L Z P Q D Z C J C L L K V
E L L T C G T O W H B I O R O
M I A B U F F O N X O S R E M
A O R U X K X N Z P X A I E Z
K G O D X V T R A S E C S A L
```

MY SCORE... OUT OF 100

MY MATE'S...

MY DAD'S...

176

Circle the odd one out in each of the boxes below — it's 20 points for each right answer!

1
NANI
NEMANJA VIDIC
CRISTIANO RONALDO
WAYNE ROONEY

2
GHANA
CAMEROON
SPAIN
NIGERIA

3
GARY LINEKER
ALAN HANSEN
ANDY TOWNSEND
MARK LAWRENSON

4
THEO WALCOTT
PETER CROUCH
JERMAIN DEFOE
AARON LENNON

5
KAKA
OTTMAR HITZFELD
RAYMOND DOMENECH
DUNGA

MY SCORE... **OUT OF 100**
MY MATE'S...
MY DAD'S...

MYSTERY MOBILE!

Which World Cup star owns this mobile phone? 50 points if you get it right!

YO LITTLE MAN! YOU'LL B WICKED 4 ENGLAND!

DUDE! STOP SHAVIN' STRIPES ON TO UR EYEBROWS!

ALRIGHT SPEEDY? HOPE UR OVER ALL UR INJURY PROBLEMS!

WONDER IF U'LL RETAIN THE TOTTENHAM PLAYER OF THE YEAR AWARD!

A.L. - UR NEW NIKE BOOTS ARE READY!

WHO IS IT?

....

MY SCORE...

OUT OF 50

MY MATE'S...

MY DAD'S...

10 QUESTIONS ON THE USA

Ten points for each correct answer!

1 Which one of these players is NOT an American goalkeeper?

- **A** Brad Friedel
- **B** Tim Howard
- **C** Julio Cesar

2 What colour is the USA home shirt?

- **A** White
- **B** Yellow
- **C** Black

3 Which USA star went on loan to Everton this season?

- **A** Eddie Johnson
- **B** Landon Donovan
- **C** Michael Bradley

4 What do they call football in the USA?

- **A** Soccer
- **B** Netball
- **C** Superbowl

5 Which one of these countries is in the USA's group at the World Cup?

- **A** Northern Ireland
- **B** England
- **C** Iceland

6 Which one of these USA internationals plays for Hull?

- **A** Marcus Hahnemann
- **B** Brad Guzan
- **C** Jozy Altidore

7 Which position does Fulham and USA star Clint Dempsey play in?

- **A** Winger
- **B** Keeper
- **C** Centre-back

8 True or false – the US were undefeated in qualifying!

- **A** True
- **B** False

9 What's the USA's nickname?

- **A** The Yanks
- **B** The Stars and Stripes
- **C** The Badgers

10 How many times have the US won the World Cup?

A 0 **B** 2 **C** 4

MY SCORE... **OUT OF 100**

MY MATE'S...

MY DAD'S...

179

WHOSE INBOX?

Guess which star is receiving these emails – 50 points if you get it right!

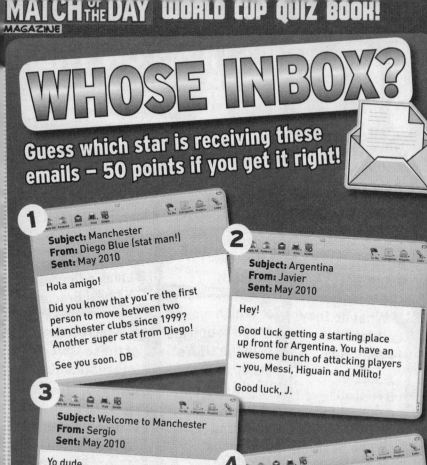

1

Subject: Manchester
From: Diego Blue (stat man!)
Sent: May 2010

Hola amigo!

Did you know that you're the first person to move between two Manchester clubs since 1999? Another super stat from Diego!

See you soon. DB

2

Subject: Argentina
From: Javier
Sent: May 2010

Hey!

Good luck getting a starting place up front for Argentina. You have an awesome bunch of attacking players – you, Messi, Higuain and Milito!

Good luck, J.

3

Subject: Welcome to Manchester
From: Sergio
Sent: May 2010

Yo dude.

I managed to get hold of that 'Welcome to Manchester' poster with you on it. Would you like it?

Let me know,
Sergio

4

Subject: Wash and go, go, go!
From: Gabriel
Sent: May 2010

Hi CT.

The local shop has shampoo on special offer – thought I'd let you know because you've got a lot of hair ;-)

G

WHO IS IT?

MY SCORE... OUT OF 50

MY MATE'S...   MY DAD'S...

TRUE OR FALSE?

Which facts are true and which are false? Get ten points for each correct answer!

1 Republic of Ireland beat Italy 1-0 at the 1994 World Cup in the USA!

True   False

2 Barcelona midfielder Andres Iniesta plays for Portugal!

True   False

3 The 2014 World Cup will be held in Brazil!

True   False

4 Birmingham midfielder Barry Ferguson plays for New Zealand!

True   False

LINK-UP PLAY

**Put a block from Group A
One's already been done**

GROUP A

ROO	RIB	
BUF	BAI	R̶O̶B̶
CRO	ALO	ESS
SKR	LEN	HOW

A	B
ROB	BEN

ARD

GROUP B

B̶E̶N̶	NSO	UCH	NEY	FON
ERY	NON	NES	TEL	IEN

5 Alan Shearer was the England captain at the 1998 World Cup!

True False

6 Fulham winger Damien Duff plays for Australia!

True False

7 Scotland have played in eight World Cup tournaments!

True False

9 Spain's home shirt is black!

True False

10 Stoke forward Tuncay plays for Uruguay!

True False

8 Brazil and have Sweden met in the World Cup more times than any other two teams!

True False

☐ MY SCORE... **OUT OF 100**
☐ MY MATE'S... ☐ MY DAD'S...

next to a block from Group B to make a player's surname.
for you — it's ten points for each correct pair you make!

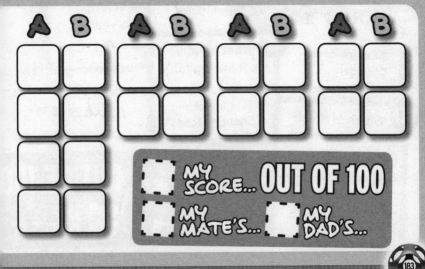

A B A B A B A B

☐ MY SCORE... **OUT OF 100**
☐ MY MATE'S... ☐ MY DAD'S...

183

NANI!

Ten points for each right answer on the superstar!

1 When did Nani last help Man. United to a Carling Cup final?

A 2010
B 2009 ✓
C 2008

2 Nani joined Man. United in 2007 from which of these clubs?

A PSV
B Sporting Lisbon ✓
C West Ham

3 How does Nani celebrate most of his goals?

A Climbing on the crossbar
B Jumping into the crowd
C Doing a somersault ✓

4 What is his shirt number at Man. United?

A 17   B 50   C 7

5 Nani picked up a red card away at which club in 2010?

A Aston Villa
B Cardiff
C Tottenham ✓

6 How many World Cups has he played in before this year?

A 0 ✓   B 2   C 4

7 Which position does Nani play in?

A Keeper
B Centre-back
C Winger

8 What is Nani most known for?

A Skills on the ball ✓
B Tough tackling
C Shouting loads

9 How old is he?

A 23 ✓   B 29   C 35

10 Which of these trophies has Nani never won?

A Champions League
B Premier League
C World Cup ✓

MY SCORE... **OUT OF 100**

MY MATE'S...   MY DAD'S...

SIL-WHO-ETTE!

**Can you identify these MOTD experts?
It's 25 points for each right answer!**

Come on West Brom!

I have a quiz at the back of MOTD mag each week!

HE'S ONE OF THE MOST-WATCHED TV PRESENTERS IN THE UK, HOSTING MOTD2 AND THE ONE SHOW!

THIS WORLD-FAMOUS COMMENTATOR STARTED WORKING FOR MATCH OF THE DAY IN 1971!

WHO IS IT?

1................

WHO IS IT?

2..................

MY SCORE... **OUT OF 50**

MY MATE'S... MY DAD'S...

185

NAME GAME!

Do you know these five players? Fill in the missing letters on their shirts – 20 points for each!

1 _ELHADJ — 3 — ALGERIA

2 KA_ _ — 10 — BRAZIL

3 D_OG_A — 11 — IVORY COAST

4 _OBBE_ — 8 — HOLLAND

5 _OR_ES — 9 — SPAIN

MY SCORE... OUT OF 100

MY MATE'S...

MY DAD'S...

MYSTERY MOBILE!

Which World Cup star owns this mobile phone? It's 50 points if you get it right!

I'VE GOT LESS HAIR ON UR HEAD THAN THE BLOKE ON MASTERCHEF!

OI, CENTRE-BACK! CAN I BORROW UR NIKE BOOTS?

GOOD LUCK OUT THERE WITH SLOVAKIA!

DO U PREFER PLAYING WITH CARRAGHER OR AGGER?

Y IS UR SHIRT NUMBER 37 AT LIVERPOOL?

WHO IS IT?

. . . .

MY SCORE...

OUT OF 50

MY MATE'S...

MY DAD'S...

CHANGING ROOM CHALLENGE!

Four top World Cup stars need to find their changing room before the match, but which of these routes will take them to it? It's 25 points for each right answer!

1 Deco **2** Andres Iniesta **3** Theo Walcott **4** Samuel Eto'o

A B C D E F

ENGLAND CAMEROON DENMARK SPAIN GERMANY PORTUGAL

MY SCORE... OUT OF 100

MY MATE'S... **MY DAD'S...**

188

DEBUT DELIGHT

Match the player to the year that they made their England debut – it's ten points for each right answer!

1 LEIGHTON BAINES

2 RIO FERDINAND

3 JERMAIN DEFOE

4 JOE HART

5 ASHLEY COLE

2008

2010

2001

2004

1997

MY SCORE... **OUT OF 50**

MY MATE'S... MY DAD'S...

CROSSWORD FUN!

Get ten points for each right answer!

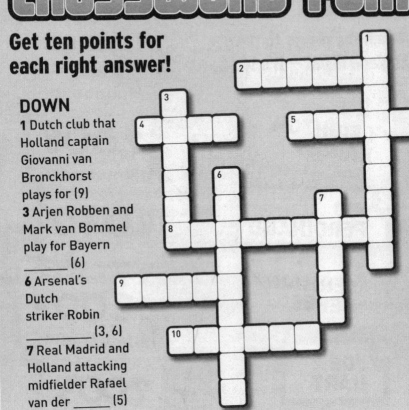

DOWN

1 Dutch club that Holland captain Giovanni van Bronckhorst plays for (9)

3 Arjen Robben and Mark van Bommel play for Bayern _____ (6)

6 Arsenal's Dutch striker Robin _____ (3, 6)

7 Real Madrid and Holland attacking midfielder Rafael van der _____ (5)

ACROSS

2 The colour of Holland's home shirt (6)

4 Surname of Liverpool's blond number 18 (4)

5 Liverpool winger Ryan _____ (5)

8 AC Milan and Holland striker Klaas-Jan _____ (9)

9 Colour of Holland's away shirt (5)

10 Inter Milan and Holland midfielder _____ Sneijder (6)

MY SCORE... **OUT OF 100**

MY MATE'S... MY DAD'S...

WHOSE INBOX?

Guess which star is receiving these emails – 50 points if you get it right!

1

Subject: South Korea captain
From: Kim
Sent: May 2010

Dear Sir,

As captain of the South Korea football team, how far do you think the side can go in this year's World Cup?

I look forward to hearing from you,
Kim

2

Subject: Midfield warrior!
From: Yeun
Sent: May 2010

Hey dude,

Good luck at the World Cup. The fact that you can play anywhere in midfield and you're a hard worker will really help the South Korean side!

All the best – Yeun

3

Subject: Man. United
From: Cho
Sent: May 2010

Hi mate!

Let me know when you're back at Man. United after the World Cup – we'll meet up. We can get Pat Evra and Daz Fletcher around my place too.

See you soon. Cho

4

Subject: ‹No subject›
From: Kong
Sent: June 2010

Yo, No.13!

Did you know this stat: you're the first Asian to ever play in a Champions League final, and the only Korean to have ever won it!

Keep up the good work. K.

WHO IS IT?

MY SCORE... OUT OF 50

MY MATE'S...

MY DAD'S...

TRUE OR FALSE?

Which facts are true and which are false? Circle the right answers – it's ten points for each one!

1 Aston Villa striker Emile Heskey plays for the USA!

True   False

2 MOTD expert Gary Lineker was the top scorer at the 1986 World Cup!

True   False

3 Man. United midfielder Anderson plays for Brazil!

True   False

4 New Zealand's nickname is the All Whites!

True   False

5 Liverpool defender Jamie Carragher plays for Australia!

True   False

6 Kolo Toure is the captain of the Ivory Coast!

True   False

7 David Beckham holds the record for having played in the most World Cups!

True   False

8 Sevilla striker Luis Fabiano plays for Brazil!

True   False

9 Algeria's home shirt has yellow and pink stripes!

True   False

10 Fulham winger Clint Dempsey plays for the USA!

True   False

MY SCORE... **OUT OF 100**

MY MATE'S...   MY DAD'S...

ANSWERS ON PAGE 232-233 (DON'T CHEAT!)

WHO AM I?

Can you work out this top star from their clues? 50 points if you're right!

WHO IS IT?

....

MY SCORE... OUT OF 50

MY MATE'S... MY DAD'S...

TIM CAHILL!

Ten points for each right answer on the superstar!

1 Which position does the Everton and Australia star play in?

A Midfield
B Goal ✓
C Defence

2 Tim's known for his...

A Leadership qualities
B Lethal headers
C Massive goal kicks ✓

3 What do Everton fans call him?

A Tiny Tim
B Tired Tim
C Tricky Tim

4 How many World Cups has he played in before this year?

A 0 **B** 1 **C** 3

5 How old is Cahill?

A 25 **B** 30 **C** 35

6 He scored Australia's first-ever...

A World Cup goal
B Goal
C Penalty

7 What shirt number does he wear for Everton?

A 6 **B** 13 **C** 17

8 Which English club did he play over 200 games for?

A Derby
B Torquay
C Millwall

9 Last year Cahill was on the losing side in which final?

A FA Cup
B Carling Cup
C Champions League

10 What is Tim's full first name?

A Timblebee
B Timothy
C Timber

 MY SCORE... **OUT OF 100**

 MY MATE'S...   MY DAD'S...

194

MYSTERY MOBILE!

Which World Cup star owns this mobile phone? It's 50 points if you get it right!

ALEX FERGUSON SAYS UR 1 OF THE BEST PLAYERS IN THE WORLD!

DON'T GET SENT OFF AT THE WORLD CUP THIS TIME!

CONGRATS ON SCORING UR 100TH PREM GOAL THIS SEASON!

SINCE RONALDO LEFT UNITED, I'VE BEEN AWESOME!

GOOD LUCK WITH ENGLAND - I WONDER WHO UR STRIKE PARTNER WILL BE!

WHO IS IT?
....

MY SCORE...
OUT OF 50
MY MATE'S...
MY DAD'S...

195

MEGA WORDSEARCH!

Can you find the 20 England legends that are hiding below? It's five points for each name you find!

Ball
Banks
Barnes
Beckham
Butcher
Charlton
Gascoigne
Hoddle
Hurst
Lineker
Matthews
Moore
Owen
Peters
Robson

M	Y	B	U	I	V	J	U	H	U	R	S	T	F	R
N	S	F	H	P	H	T	A	J	J	M	V	D	O	D
O	O	H	E	N	G	I	O	C	S	A	G	B	X	F
W	G	T	I	X	X	J	K	R	P	Z	S	G	F	G
E	Q	U	L	L	D	L	C	E	O	O	L	S	X	A
N	V	E	M	R	T	N	Q	H	N	J	L	R	C	Q
W	F	J	O	B	A	O	N	C	Q	F	A	E	D	S
A	S	N	O	B	P	H	N	T	Y	C	B	T	W	Z
D	T	A	R	E	L	O	C	U	E	M	S	E	V	X
D	I	M	E	C	S	I	T	B	C	C	H	P	H	O
L	L	A	L	K	E	R	N	E	I	T	E	K	H	B
E	E	E	D	H	N	H	C	E	T	I	A	H	F	D
N	S	S	D	A	R	Q	S	A	K	Y	R	A	M	E
F	F	H	O	M	A	H	M	K	T	E	E	X	R	N
O	P	L	H	K	B	S	K	N	A	B	R	H	Y	O

Seaman
Shearer
Shilton

Stiles
Waddle

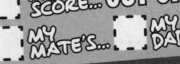

MY SCORE... OUT OF 100

MY MATE'S...

MY DAD'S...

196

SQUAD SELECTION!

Tick the players who have been to previous World Cups and cross those who haven't – it's ten points for each!

1 ASHLEY COLE

Been to a World Cup? ☐

2 STEPHEN WARNOCK

Been to a World Cup? ☐

3 JOE HART

Been to a World Cup? ☐

4 WAYNE ROONEY

Been to a World Cup? ☐

5 STEVEN GERARRD

Been to a World Cup? ☐

☐ MY SCORE... OUT OF 50

☐ MY MATE'S... ☐ MY DAD'S...

ODD ONE OUT!

Circle the odd one out in each of the boxes below – get 20 points for each right answer!

1
- 2007 COPA AMERICA
- EURO 2008
- 2009 FA CUP
- 2010 WORLD CUP

2
- ALGERIA
- USA
- SLOVENIA
- HOLLAND

3
- JOHN TERRY
- MAXI RODRIGUEZ
- STEVEN GERRARD
- DANIEL AGGER

4
- PENALTY SPOT
- SHORTS
- HALF-WAY LINE
- PENALTY AREA

5
- F50i TUNiT
- PREDATOR_X
- DIY EAGLE-TRON
- CTR360 MAESTRI

MY SCORE... **OUT OF 100**

MY MATE'S...

MY DAD'S...

TEAM BUSCHALLENGE!

Four top World Cup stars are late for a game, but which route will lead them to the correct team bus? It's 25 points for each one you get right!

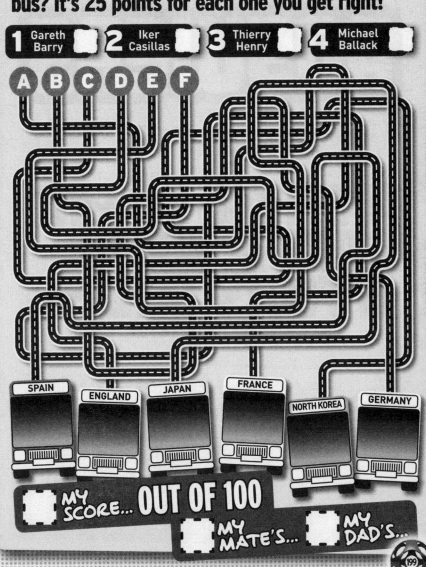

MY SCORE... **OUT OF 100**

MY MATE'S...   MY DAD'S...

199

ANSWERS

IT'S TIME TO FIND OUT IF YOU'RE A FOOTY GENIUS!

P6 - MYSTERY MOBILE!
Glen Johnson

P6-7 - TEAM SHEET!
1 Green, 2 Liverpool, 3 Rio, 4 Barry, 5 Aaron, 6 ST,
7 James, 8 Capello, 9 Everton, 10 Clint

P8 - MESSI!
1 B, 2 A, 3 B, 4 B, 5 B, 6 C, 7 C, 8 A, 9 B, 10 B

P9 - SIL-WHO-ETTE!
1 Gary Lineker, 2 Lee Dixon

P10 - MEGA WORDSEARCH!

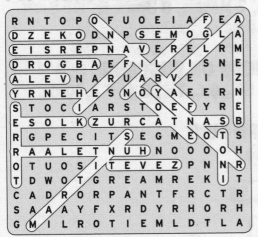

P11 - TRANSFER CONNECT!
1 Ronaldo - £80m, 2 Gianluigi Buffon - £32m,
3 Glen Johnson - £18m, 4 Carlos Tevez - £25m

P12 - PREM LINK!
1 Arsenal, **2** Fulham, **3** Man. City, **4** Everton,
5 Liverpool, **6** Portsmouth, **7** Tottenham,
8 Chelsea, **9** Man. United, **10** Hull

P13 - NAME GAME!
1 Lampard, **2** Iniesta, **3** Benzema , **4** Deco,
5 K. Toure

P14-15 - WAYNE ROONEY!
1 B, **2** B, **3** A, **4** C, **5** A, **6** A, **7** B, **8** A, **9** C, **10** C

P14-15 - JUMBLED UP!
1 Portugal, **2** Chile, **3** Greece , **4** England,
5 France, **6** Japan, **7** Mexico, **8** Uruguay,
9 USA, **10** North Korea

P16 - 10 QUESTIONS ON ENGLAND!
1 C, **2** C, **3** A, **4** B, **5** B, **6** C, **7** C, **8** A, **9** A, **10** C

P17 - CROSSWORD FUN!

P18-19 - 10 QUESTIONS ON SPAIN!
1 B, 2 C, 3 B, 4 A, 5 C, 6 B, 7 A, 8 C, 9 A, 10 A

P18-19 - COUNTRY CONNECT!
1 F, 2 I, 3 J, 4 E, 5 H, 6 B, 7 C, 8 A, 9 G, 10 D

P20 - TEAM BUS CHALLENGE!
1 F, 2 D, 3 A, 4 E

P21 - NICKNAME CONNECT!
1 D, 2 A, 3 B, 4 E, 5 C

P22 - CRISTIANO RONALDO!
1 B, 2 A, 3 B, 4 B, 5 A, 6 B, 7 B, 8 A, 9 A, 10 B

P23 - WHO AM I?
Nicklas Bendtner

P24 - TEAM SHEET!
1 Inter, 2 Alves, 3 Real Madrid, 4 ST, 5 Man. City,
6 Emmanuel, 7 Yaya, 8 Chelsea, 9 ST, 10 Drogba

P25 - CROSSWORD FUN!

P26 - TRUE OR FALSE!
1 False, 2 True, 3 False, 4 True, 5 True, 6 True,
7 False, 8 False, 9 True, 10 True

P27 - QUALIFIED?
1 No, 2 Yes, 3 Yes, 4 No, 5 No, 6 Yes, 7 No,
8 No, 9 Yes, 10 No

P28 - DADS v LADS!
1990 - 1 Rome, 2 Terry Butcher, 3 Rep. of Ireland,
Holland, Egypt, 4 West Germany, 5 Peter Shilton
NOW - 1 South Africa, 2 Rio Ferdinand, 3 USA,
Algeria, Slovenia, 4 Italy, 5 David James

P29 - NAME GAME!
1 Rooney, 2 Fabiano, 3 Carvalho,
4 Cannavaro, 5 Xavi

P30 - DIDIER DROGBA!
1 A, 2 C, 3 B, 4 A, 5 A, 6 B, 7 C, 8 A, 9 C, 10 B

P31 - MYSTERY MOBILE!
Rio Ferdinand

P32 - MEGA WORDSEARCH!

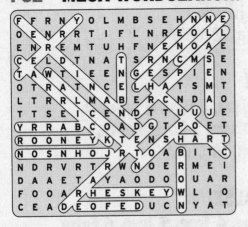

P33 - ODD ONE OUT!
1 Gareth Barry (He is only midfielder), 2 Fabio Capello (He is the only manager), 3 1-2-7 (It's not a proper formation), 4 Michael Ballack (He is the only German), 5 Rio Ferdinand (He is the only defender)

P34 - SIL-WHO-ETTE!
1 Alan Hansen, 2 Mark Bright

P35 - SOUTH AFRICA GUIDE!
1 B, 2 B, 3 A, 4 C, 5 C

P36 - FERNANDO TORRES!
1 C, 2 B, 3 B, 4 B, 5 B, 6 C, 7 A, 8 A, 9 C, 10 A

P37 - RAPPING ROWS!
1 Green, 2 Queen, 3 Fourteen,
4 Barry, 5 Gary, 6 Harry,
7 Ribery, 8 Messi, 9 Henry,
10 Capello, 11 Ronaldo, 12 Yellow

P38 - PREM LINK!
1 Man. United, 2 Chelsea, 3 Hull, 4 Arsenal,
5 Man. City, 6 Tottenham, 7 Portsmouth,
8 Liverpool, 9 Fulham, 10 Stoke

P39 - TRUE OR FALSE!
1 True, 2 False, 3 True, 4 True, 5 True, 6 False,
7 False, 8 True, 9 False, 10 False

P40-41 - 10 QUESTIONS ON BRAZIL!
1 A, 2 B, 3 A, 4 C, 5 A, 6 C, 7 C, 8 A, 9 B, 10 B

P40-41 - COUNTRY CONNECT!
1 J, 2 G, 3 A, 4 F, 5 B, 6 C, 7 D, 8 I, 9 H, 10 E

P42 - WHOSE INBOX?
Cesc Fabregas

P43 - SHOOTING PRACTICE!
1 Paraguay, **2** Old Lady, **3** Ribery, **4** Terry,
5 Uruguay, **6** Germany, **7** Ashley, **8** Ledley
Outer-ring country: Portugal

P44 - CROSSWORD FUN!

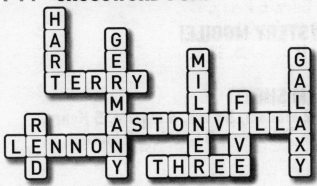

P45 - ROBIN VAN PERSIE!
1 C, **2** B, **3** A, **4** A, **5** A, **6** A, **7** B, **8** A, **9** C, **10** A

P46 - TEAM KIT CHALLENGE!
1 E, **2** B, **3** A, **4** C

P47 - SQUAD SELECTION!
1 Yes, **2** No, **3** Yes, **4** No , **5** Yes

P48 - WHO AM I?
Tim Howard

P49 - DADS v LADS!

1986 - 1 Argentina, **2** Mexico, **3** Morocco, Poland, Portugal, **4** Sir Bobby Robson, **5** Diego Maradona

NOW - 1 Spain, **2** Adrian Chiles, **3** Ukraine, Croatia, Belarus, Kazakhstan, Andorra, **4** 63, **5** Frank Lampard

P50 - MYSTERY MOBILE!

Deco

P51 - TEAM SHEET!

1 Arsenal, **2** William, **3** Evra, **4** Madrid, **5** Henry, **6** Barcelona, **7** Nicolas, **8** Chelsea, **9** Florent, **10** Arsenal

P52 - AARON LENNON!

1 A, **2** B, **3** B, **4** A, **5** A, **6** C, **7** C, **8** A, **9** B, **10** B

P53 - JOIN THE DOTS!

P54 - MEGA WORDSEARCH!

P55 - COOL FINISHING!

1. FREE-KICK
2. PENALTY
3. FULL-TIME
4. ENGLAND
5. TROPHY
6. OFFSIDE
7. REFEREE
8. LINESMAN
9. HALF-TIME
10. SUPPORTER

P56 - NAME GAME!
1 Rodriguez, 2 Terry, 3 Henry,
4 Buffon, 5 Sneijder

P57 - DEFENSIVE DUOS!
1 William Gallas - Eric Abidal, 2 Lucio - Luisao
3 Emmanuel Eboue - Kolo Toure,
4 Giorgio Chiellini - Fabio Cannavaro,
5 Carlos Puyol - Carlos Marchena

P58 - CARLOS TEVEZ!

1 B, 2 C, 3 A, 4 C, 5 C, 6 A, 7 B, 8 B, 9 B, 10 A

P59 - LINK-UP PLAY!

MIL-NER, WIN-GER, GRE-ECE, REP-LAY, GRO-UPS,
TOR-RES, SER-BIA, DRO-GBA, KEE-PER, CAH-ILL

P60 - WHOSE INBOX?

Steven Gerrard

P61 - PREM LINK!

1 Chelsea, 2 West Ham, 3 Man. United, 4 Burnley,
5 Fulham, 6 Liverpool, 7 Wigan,
8 Blackburn, 9 Everton, 10 Arsenal

P62-63 - 10 QUESTIONS ON HOLLAND!

1 C, 2 A, 3 A, 4 B, 5 A, 6 C, 7 A, 8 B, 9 B, 10 A

P62-63 - TRUE OR FALSE!

1 False, 2 False, 3 True, 4 True, 5 True, 6 False,
7 True, 8 False, 9 True, 10 True

P64 - CROSSWORD FUN!

P65 - WHO AM I?
Wilson Palacios

P66 - JAMES MILNER!
1 A, **2** B, **3** B, **4** A, **5** C, **6** A, **7** B, **8** C, **9** A, **10** A

P67 - JUMBLED UP!
1 Italy, **2** Ivory Coast, **3** Brazil , **4** Serbia,
5 Ghana, **6** Argentina, **7** Algeria, **8** Honduras,
9 Australia, **10** Slovenia

P68 - WORLD CUP WINNERS!
1 Yes, **2** Yes, **3** No , **4** No, **5** Yes, **6** No, **7** Yes,
8 No, **9** No, **10** Yes

P69 - HIDDEN PLAYER!

Hidden player - Casillas

P70 - MYSTERY MOBILE!
William Gallas

P71 - DADS v LADS!
1994 - 1 Terry Venables, **2** Brazil v Italy,
3 Los Angeles, **4** Dunga, **5** Holland
NOW - 1 False, **2** Spain or Holland, **3** Johannesburg,
4 Iker Casillas, **5** France

P72-73 - QUALIFIED?
1 No, **2** No, **3** Yes, **4** No, **5** Yes, **6** Yes, **7** No, **8** No,
9 Yes, **10** Yes

P72-73 - WHAT COUNTRY?
1 E, **2** I, **3** F, **4** G, **5** D, **6** J, **7** B, **8** H, **9** C, **10** A

P74 - DAVID VILLA!
1 C, 2 B, 3 B, 4 C, 5 A, 6 C, 7 A, 8 C, 9 A, 10 B

P75 - NAME GAME!
1 Hulk, 2 A. Cole, 3 Song, 4 De Jong, 5 Nani

P76 - MEGA WORDSEARCH!

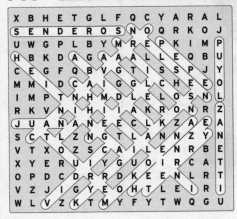

P77 - SQUAD SELECTION!
1 Yes, 2 Yes, 3 No, 4 Yes, 5 No

P78 - WHO AM I?
Samir Nasri

P79 - 10 QUESTIONS ON FRANCE!
1 A, 2 A, 3 B, 4 C, 5 C, 6 B, 7 B, 8 A, 9 B, 10 C

P80 - WHOSE INBOX?
Michael Ballack

213

P81 - SHADY PIC!

P82 - RIO FERDINAND!
1 C, **2** B, **3** B, **4** A, **5** B, **6** C, **7** A, **8** B, **9** C, **10** C

P83 - SIL-WHO-ETTE!
1 Mark Lawrenson, **2** Martin Keown

P84 - TEAM SHEET!
1 Tottenham, **2** Alexandre, **3** Samuel, **4** Milan,
5 Man. City, **6** Inter, **7** Kuyt, **8** Bayern Munich,
9 Van, **10** Arsenal

P85 - CROSSWORD FUN!

P86 - TRUE OR FALSE!
1 True, 2 True, 3 False, 4 True, 5 True, 6 True,
7 False, 8 False, 9 True, 10 True

P87 - NAME GAME!
1 Ferdinand, 2 Lahm, 3 Essien, 4 Kuyt,
5 Casillas

P88 - CHANGING ROOM CHALLENGE!
1 D, 2 C, 3 E, 4 A

P89 - COOL FINISHING!

P90 - KAKA!

1 A, 2 A, 3 C, 4 B, 5 B, 6 A, 7 A, 8 C, 9 C, 10 B

P91 - MYSTERY MOBILE!

Fernando Torres

P92 - TRUE OR FALSE!

1 False, 2 False, 3 False, 4 True, 5 True, 6 True, 7 True, 8 True, 9 False, 10 False

P93 - LINK-UP PLAY!

WEM-BLEY, GER-MANY, PEN-ALTY, DEN-MARK, REF-EREE, HOL-LAND, WHI-STLE, ALG-ERIA, DEF-ENCE, URU-GUAY, STR-IKER

P94 - HIDDEN PLAYERS!

Hidden team - Cameroon

P95 - WHO AM I?
Nani

P96-97 - FRANK LAMPARD!
1 A, 2 C, 3 B, 4 C, 5 A, 6 B, 7 C, 8 A, 9 B, 10 B

P96-97 - RAPPING ROWS!
1 Free, 2 Lee, 3 Wembley, 4 Cole, 5 Goal,
6 Cole, 7 Uruguay, 8 Kai, 9 Paraguay,
10 C, 11 Rooney, 12 Germany

P98 - MEGA WORDSEARCH!

P99 - ODD ONE OUT!
1 Wayne Rooney (He is the only Man. United player),
2 Nicklas Bendtner (He is the only striker),
3 Ghana (The only non-European country),
4 Holland (They haven't won the World Cup),
5 Italy (The other teams play in green)

P100 - 10 QUESTIONS ON ARGENTINA!
1 A, 2 A, 3 B, 4 B, 5 C, 6 A, 7 C, 8 B, 9 C, 10 B

P101 - NAME GAME!
1 Messi, 2 Maicon, 3 Johnson, 4 Mikel, 5 Park

P102 - WHOSE INBOX?
Nemanja Vidic

P103 - JOIN THE DOTS!

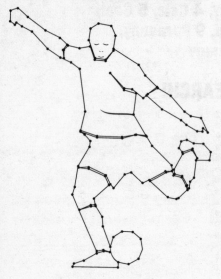

P104 - STEVEN GERRARD!
1 A, 2 C, 3 A, 4 B, 5 B, 6 A, 7 B, 8 B, 9 A, 10 A

P105 - JUMBLED UP!
1 Cameroon, 2 Switzerland, 3 Holland,
4 South Africa, 5 Nigeria, 6 Spain,
7 Denmark, 8 New Zealand,
9 Paraguay, 10 South Korea

P106 - CROSSWORD FUN!

P107 - WHO AM I?
Ashley Cole

P108 - MIDFIELD MAESTROS!
1 Thomas Hitzlsperger – Michael Ballack, **2** John Obi Mikel – Dickson Etuhu, **3** Daniele De Rossi – Andrea Pirlo, **4** Nigel de Jong – Wesley Sneijder,
5 Lassana Diarra – Yoann Gourcuff

P109 - HIDDEN COUNTRY!

Hidden country - Portugal

P110-111 - QUALIFIED?
1 Yes, **2** No, **3** No, **4** Yes, **5** No, **6** Yes, **7** No, **8** No,
9 Yes, **10** Yes

P110-111 - TRUE OR FALSE!
1 True, **2** True, **3** True, **4** False, **5** False, **6** True,
7 True, **8** False, **9** False, **10** True

P112 - MYSTERY MOBILE!
Patrice Evra

P113 - THIERRY HENRY!
1 B, **2** C, **3** C, **4** A, **5** A, **6** B, **7** B, **8** C, **9** A, **10** C

P114 - DADS v LADS!
1990 - **1** False, **2** Argentina, **3** Salvatore Schillaci,
4 Fourth, **5** Group stages
NOW - **1** Yes, **2** France, **3** Nine, **4** First,
5 Holland, Iceland, Norway or Macedonia

P115 - SUPER STRIKERS!
1 Carlos Tevez – Gonzalo Higuain, **2** Robinho – Luis
Fabiano, **3** Nicklas Bendtner – Jon Dahl Tomasson,
4 Thierry Henry – Nicolas Anelka,
5 Fernando Torres – David Villa

P116-117 - 10 QUESTIONS ON PORTUGAL!
1 A, **2** A, **3** A, **4** C, **5** B, **6** B, **7** C, **8** B, **9** A, **10** B

P116-117 - COUNTRY CONNECT!
1 C, 2 F, 3 E, 4 J, 5 H, 6 D, 7 G, 8 A, 9 I, 10 B

P118 - MEGA WORDSEARCH!

P119 - DEBUT DELIGHT!
1 D, 2 A, 3 E, 4 C, 5 B

P120 - CESC FABREGAS!
1 B, 2 A, 3 A, 4 A, 5 B, 6 B, 7 B, 8 C, 9 B, 10 A

P121 - PREM LINK!
1 Tottenham, 2 Arsenal, 3 Liverpool, 4 Fulham,
5 Man. City, 6 Chelsea, 7 West Ham,
8 Everton, 9 Man. United, 10 Hull

P122 - TEAM FOOD CHALLENGE!
1 C, 2 B, 3 E, 4 A

P123 - ODD ONE OUT!
1 Switzerland (The other three are national nicknames),
2 Peter Crouch (He doesn't play for Everton),
3 Hugo Rodallega (He doesn't play for England),
4 Levi's (The other three make kits),
5 Mighty Twig (The others are names of football boots)

P124 - WHOSE INBOX?
Didier Drogba

P125 - CROSSWORD FUN!

P126 - SIL-WHO-ETTE!
1 Alan Shearer, **2** Les Ferdinand

P127 - SAMUEL ETO'O!
1 B, **2** A, **3** A, **4** A, **5** C, **6** C, **7** C, **8** A, **9** C, **10** B

P128-129 - TRUE OR FALSE!
1 False, **2** True, **3** False, **4** True, **5** False, **6** True,
7 True, **8** False, **9** True, **10** True

P128-129 - QUALIFIED?
1 No, **2** Yes, **3** Yes, **4** No, **5** No, **6** Yes, **7** Yes,
8 No, **9** Yes, **10** No

P130 - 10 QUESTIONS ON ITALY!
1 A, **2** A, **3** A, **4** C, **5** B, **6** C, **7** B, **8** B, **9** A, **10** C

P131 - NAME GAME!
1 Gallas, **2** Schweinsteiger, **3** Pirlo,
4 Vidic, **5** Kalou

P132 - WORLD CUP WINNERS!
1 Yes, **2** No, **3** Yes, **4** Yes, **5** No, **6** No, **7** Yes,
8 No, **9** Yes, **10** No

P133 - WHO AM I?
Dirk Kuyt

P134-135 - JOHN TERRY!
1 C, **2** A, **3** B, **4** B, **5** A, **6** B, **7** B, **8** C, **9** C, **10** A

P134-135 - LINK-UP PLAY!
FABR-EGAS, AQUI-LANI, FOOT-BALL, PORT-UGAL,
CAME-ROON, SLOV-AKIA, PARA-GUAY, MIDF-IELD,
CROS-SBAR, CASI-LLAS

P136 - TEAM SHEET!
1 Inter, **2** Bayern, **3** Mascherano, **4** Liverpool,
5 Lionel, **6** Barcelona, **7** Man. City, **8** Everton,
9 Mikel, **10** Everton

P137 - MYSTERY MOBILE!
Gareth Barry

P138 - MEGA WORDSEARCH!

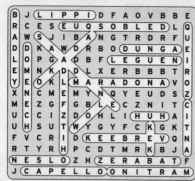

P139 - GUESS THE AGE!
1 D, 2 A, 3 B, 4 E, 5 C

P140 - JOIN THE DOTS!

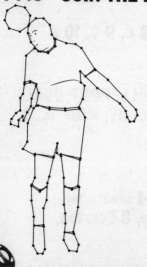

P141 - WHO AM I?
Clint Dempsey

P142 - ROBINHO!
1 A, 2 C, 3 B, 4 C, 5 A,
6 B, 7 B, 8 C, 9 C, 10 A

P143 - JUMBLED UP!
1 Ferdinand, 2 Crouch,
3 Terry, 4 Cole,
5 Barry, 6 Lampard,
7 Rooney, 8 Gerrard,
9 Defoe, 10 Lennon

P144 - NAME GAME!
1 Barry, 2 Anelka,
3 Villa, 4 Donovan,
5 Skrtel

P145 - DADS v LADS!
1994 - 1 Romario, 2 USA, 3 Sweden,
4 Ray Houghton, 5 Did not qualify
NOW - 1 Luis Fabiano, 2 Clint Dempsey,
3 Denmark, 4 Lippi, 5 John Terry

P146 - TRUE OR FALSE!
1 True, 2 True, 3 False, 4 True, 5 False,
6 False, 7 True, 8 False, 9 True, 10 False

P147 - WHOSE INBOX?
Nicolas Anelka

P148 - TEAM BUS CHALLENGE!
1 B, 2 F, 3 E, 4 A

P149 - ODD ONE OUT!
1 David Beckham (The others are managers),
2 David Villa (The others all captain their country),
3 Robert Huth (The others all play for Chelsea),
4 Wembley (The others are venues for the 2010 World Cup),
5 Matthew Upson (The others are strikers)

P150 - FRANCK RIBERY!
1 A, **2** C, **3** A, **4** B, **5** C, **6** B, **7** A, **8** B, **9** C, **10** C

P151 - WHOSE INBOX?
Pepe Reina

P152 - TRUE OR FALSE!
1 True, **2** False, **3** False, **4** True, **5** True, **6** False,
7 True, **8** True, **9** True, **10** True

P153 - QUALIFIED?
1 Yes, **2** No, **3** No, **4** Yes, **5** No, **6** No, **7** No,
8 Yes, **9** Yes, **10** Yes

P154-155 - 10 QUESTIONS ON GERMANY!
1 A, **2** A, **3** B, **4** C, **5** B, **6** C, **7** A, **8** B, **9** A, **10** A

P154-155 - RAPPING ROWS!
1 City, **2** Persie, **3** Xavi, **4** Mark, **5** Park,
6 Dark, **7** Cannavaro, **8** Mexico, **9** Defoe,
10 Italy, **11** Behrami, **12** Chile

P156 - WHO AM I?
Bacary Sagna

P157 - COUNTRY CONNECT!
1 F, 2 A, 3 J, 4 B, 5 C, 6 H, 7 E, 8 D, 9 I, 10 G

P158 - GARETH BARRY!
1 B, 2 A, 3 C, 4 C, 5 A, 6 B, 7 A, 8 C, 9 C, 10 B

P159 - MYSTERY MOBILE!
Frank Lampard

P160 - MEGA WORDSEARCH!

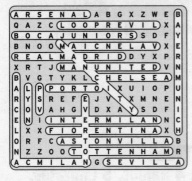

P161 - COOL FINISHING!

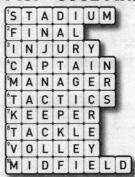

1. STADIUM
2. FINAL
3. INJURY
4. CAPTAIN
5. MANAGER
6. TACTICS
7. KEEPER
8. TACKLE
9. VOLLEY
10. MIDFIELD

P162 - SHADY PIC!

P163 - TEAM SHEET!
1 Casillas, **2** Real Madrid, **3** Barcelona, **4** Real,
5 Andres, **6** Fernando, **7** Liverpool, **8** Valencia,
9 Cesc, **10** West Ham

P164 - WHO AM I?
Steven Pienaar

P165 - SHOOTING PRACTICE!
1 Fouls, **2** Andres, **3** Baines, **4** Ramos, **5** Emirates,
6 Gallas, **7** Alves, **8** Spurs
Outer-ring name: Fabregas

P166 - JAVIER MASCHERANO!
1 C, **2** A, **3** A, **4** B, **5** C, **6** A, **7** B, **8** A, **9** C, **10** C

P167 - CROSSWORD FUN!

P168 - WHOSE INBOX?
Robin van Persie

P169 - PREM LINK!
1 Chelsea, 2 Aston Villa, 3 Liverpool,
4 Wigan, 5 Arsenal, 6 Stoke, 7 Everton,
8 Man. United, 9 West Ham, 10 Wolves

P170-171 - LINK-UP PLAY!
LAM-PARD, RON-ALDO, ROB-INHO, CAP-ELLO,
FAB-IANO, DEM-PSEY, JOH-NSON, GER-RARD,
INI-ESTA, BAL-LACK

P170-171 - COUNTRY CONNECT!
1 C, 2 G, 3 B, 4 J, 5 D, 6 A, 7 I, 8 F, 9 H, 10 E

P172 - TEAM KIT CHALLENGE!
1 A, 2 E, 3 C, 4 B

P173 - TRANSFER CONNECT!
1 James Milner - £12.5m, **2** Robinho - £32.5m,
3 Nemanja Vidic - £7m, **4** Sotirios Kyrgiakos - £2m

P174-175 - GIANLUIGI BUFFON!
1 A, **2** B, **3** A, **4** A, **5** C, **6** B, **7** C, **8** A, **9** B, **10** B

P174-175 - JUMBLED UP!
1 Torres, **2** Fabregas, **3** Ballack, **4** Anelka,
5 Van Persie, **6** Robinho, **7** Ronaldo, **8** Messi,
9 Tevez, **10** Drogba

P176 - MEGA WORDSEARCH!

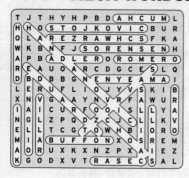

P177 - ODD ONE OUT!
1 Cristiano Ronaldo (The others play for Man. United),
2 Spain (The others are African nations),
3 Andy Townsend (The others are BBC experts),
4 Theo Walcott (The others play for Tottenham),
5 Kaka (The others are managers)

P178 - MYSTERY MOBILE!
Aaron Lennon

P179 - 10 QUESTIONS ON USA!
1 C, 2 A, 3 B, 4 A, 5 B, 6 C, 7 A, 8 B, 9 A, 10 A

P180 - WHOSE INBOX?
Carlos Tevez

P181 - QUALIFIED?
1 Yes, 2 No, 3 No, 4 No, 5 Yes, 6 No, 7 Yes,
8 No, 9 No, 10 Yes

P182-183 - TRUE OR FALSE!
1 True, 2 False, 3 True, 4 False, 5 True, 6 False,
7 True, 8 True, 9 False, 10 False

P182-183 - LINK-UP PLAY!
ROO-NEY, RIB-ERY, BUF-FON, BAI-NES, CRO-UCH,
ALO-NSO, ESS-IEN, SKR-TEL, LEN-NON, HOW-ARD

P184 - NANI!
1 A, 2 B, 3 C, 4 A, 5 A, 6 A, 7 C, 8 A, 9 A, 10 C

P185 - SIL-WHO-ETTE!
1 Adrian Chiles, 2 John 'Motty' Motson

P186 - NAME GAME!
1 Belhadj, 2 Kaka, 3 Drogba,
4 Robben, 5 Torres

P187 - MYSTERY MOBILE!
Martin Skrtel

P188 - CHANGING ROOM CHALLENGE!
1 E, 2 C, 3 D, 4 A

P189 - DEBUT DELIGHT!
1 B, 2 E, 3 D, 4 A, 5 C

P190 - CROSSWORD FUN!

P191 - WHOSE INBOX?
Park Ji-Sung

P192 - TRUE OR FALSE!
1 False, 2 True, 3 True, 4 True, 5 False, 6 False, 7 False, 8 True, 9 False, 10 True

P193 - WHO AM I?
Salomon Kalou

P194 - TIM CAHILL!
1 A, 2 B, 3 A, 4 B, 5 B, 6 A, 7 C, 8 C, 9 A, 10 B

P195 - MYSTERY MOBILE!
Wayne Rooney

P196 - MEGA WORDSEARCH!

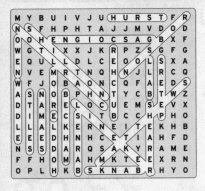

P197 - SQUAD SELECTION!
1 Yes, 2 No, 3 No, 4 Yes, 5 Yes

P198 - ODD ONE OUT!
1 2009 FA Cup
(The others are
international
tournaments),
2 Holland
(The others are
all in England's
World Cup group),
3 John Terry
(The other internationals
play for Liverpool),
4 Shorts
(The others are parts
of a football pitch),
5 DIY Eagle-Tron
(The others are real
names of football boots)

P199 - TEAM BUS
CHALLENGE!
1 A, 2 D, 3 F, 4 B

NOTES!